Diabeti

Bread & Breakfast

M000033869

David Maxwell

Contents

About This Book

Food is one of the most primal and greatest pleasures we enjoy. Restrictions on what you can and cannot eat can greatly limit that pleasure. Diabetes is a condition that leads to such restrictions, and if you don't know a way around the restrictions to still enjoy great food, life can become... well, kinda bland. Don't worry though, since you've picked this book up, you've taken your first steps towards enjoying insanely delicious food that complies with a diabetic's nutritional restricitons.

This book will bring you numerous insanely delicious recipes, and each recipe is followed by a detailed list of nutritional contents to remove guesswork and allow you to know exactly what is going inside you!

Interpreting the Nutritional Info

In the recipes section, quite a few recipes will contain ingredients marked as "optional", or "to taste", or "a dash". There is no way to give a definite nutritional content when I do not know If and how much of these ingredients you will be using. So, the nutritional info section will simply omit the nutritional content of these ingredients, so plan these ingredients carefully.

You will also find ingredients with alternatives. In this case, the Nutritional info will hold true if you use the first choice of ingredients.

In some cases, you will find that a range of the ingredient can be used instead of a set amount. In this case, the nutritional info will hold true if you use the lowest end (the first number) of the range.

In quite a few recipes, you will find ingredients listed as "serve with" right at the end of the recipes. These ingredients will also not contribute to the "nutritional info" section.

There are recipes that call for cooked rice, pasta, and other grains. The nutritional info will contain the grain itself, but not the oil, salt, and other stuff that might have been used to cook the ingredients.

There are tips and variations given for a few of the recipes. Just know that the nutritional info will not contain the content of these tips and variations.

Many of the recipes also contain meat ingredients. In order to incorporate these in the nutritional info, I'll assume that all meat was skinless and all visible fat was removed before cooking. The.

Tips for Healthier, Happier Eating
How to Plan Healthy Meals

Mean planning is indispensable for diabetics. If you suffer from diabetes, you should have a mean planning stipulating what to eat, when to eat, and how much to eat. As every person has a different body and requirements, it is best to consult a registered dietician to have a meal plan prepared that caters exactly to your needs. Here are the tools you will need when planning a meal plan:-

1. **Exchange List:** An exchange list is a list of foods that are categorized together as they have similar carbohydrate, protein, and fat content. All food items on an exchange list can be substituted for another item on the same exchange list. Variety is the spice of life, and exchange lists make sure you have plenty of options when following a diet plan.

2. **Carbohydrate counting:** As a diabetic, carbohydrates are the primary nutrient you need to watch out for. Simply put, carbohydrate counting is the practice of counting carbohydrates in the food to help you manage your blood glucose. Most food items come with a nutritional fact label that specifies the amount of carbohydrates in that particular food item. When in doubt, feel free to talk to your dietician. It is useful because carbohydrates are the main nutrient in food that affects blood glucose.

3. **Create Your Plate:** The "Create Your Plate" technique helps people with diabetes create meals with uniformly distributed carbohydrate content and precise portion sizes. This is one of the simplest meal-planning options as it does not call for any special stuff—you just need a plate. Fill half of your plate with non-starchy vegetables, like as

spinach, carrots, cabbage, green beans, or broccoli. Fill one-fourth of the plate with starchy foods, such as rice, pasta, beans, or peas. Fill the remaining portion of your plate with meat or a meat substitute, such as cheese with less than 3 grams of fat per ounce, cottage cheese, or egg substitute. For a balanced meal, put in a serving of low-fat or non-fat milk and a serving of fruit.

Feel free to use any of the three tools mentioned above. Just make sure you have a meal plan. It is vital to manage your blood glucose levels, improve cholesterol levels, and maintain a healthy blood pressure and a healthy body weight. Once you have a good diet plan, you can easily prevent, or control diabetes.

Learning Portion Control

The diet plan tells you how much to eat. However, to actually eat the stipulated amount, you will need to learn to measure and weigh your ingredients. Once you start doing it, you will get better, faster, and more accurate at it with time, until it starts coming to you naturally.

If you're a beginner who has no idea approximately potion control, don't worry, I got you covered. Remember that tablespoons and teaspoons will only give you approximate measurements. You will need to prepare a potion control toolbox to get started. Here is what you'll be putting in it:

- Measuring spoons for ½ teaspoon, 1 teaspoon, ½ tablespoon, and 1 tablespoon
- A see-through 1-cup measuring cup with markings at ¼, ⅓, ½, ⅔, and ¾ cup
- Measuring cups for dry ingredients, including ¼ ⅓, ½, and 1 cup.

You probably already have a few of these in your kitchen. If not, they are quite easy to find in markets and online stores. Place these tools where you can grab them easily, as you'll be using these multiple times in a day.

From time to time, you will also find ingredients that are measured by weight. For these, it is always a good idea to have a inexpensive food scale in your kitchen. You may already have most of these in your kitchen.

When weighing meat, poultry, and seafood, keep in mind that the cooked quantity of meat always weighs less than the quantity initially taken as the water in the meat evaporates. For example, you will need 4 ounces of raw, boneless meat, or 5 ounces of raw meat with the bone—to get 3 cooked ounces. Approximately 4½ ounces of raw chicken (with the bone and skin) gives 3 ounces cooked. Make sure you remove the skin from the chicken before cooking it.

Other than using measuring and potion control at the time of cooking, there are other ways of controlling your intake. I've mentioned a few of these below.:

- Eating on small plates and bowls can make less food seem like more, which gives you a psychological edge.
- Use measuring cups to serve food to effortlessly regulate how much you're serving and eating.
- Know how much your drinking glasses and bowls can hold, so you have an idea how much you're drinking or eating when you fill them.
- Try not to serve your meals family-style because leaving big serving dishes on the table can lead to second helpings and overeating.
- Avoid over-buying. Keep in mind how much you need to prepare the recipe and buy just that much.

When you're out, and do not have access to your potion control kit, you will need to rely on estimation to fit your diet plan. It is usually a good idea to figure out how much your hand can hold while you have access to your potion control kit. Take a table spoon and put it on your thumb to see what it looks like. Similarly, you can get a idea of how much teaspoons, tablespoons, ounces, and cups are with regard to your own hand. Note what an ounce looks and feels like on your palm.

There is no one way to do it. When you have access to your kit, feel free to hold most commonly used amounts in your own hands to get an idea of how much looks like what on your fingers or palm or thumb. Once you get the hand of it, you will approximately be able to fit your diet plan even when you're away from home and do not have access to your tools. Remember that the more you weigh and measure your foods at home, the easier it will be to get an idea of portions on the road.

Controlling your portions when you eat at a restaurant can be tricky. It is usually a good idea to get an idea approximately how much quantity you will get in the dishes. The waiter will probably be happy to help you out with that. However, it is impossible to control what ingredients they put in there, so be careful. Also, it is easy to get carried away in all-you-can-eat buffets, so it is a good idea to avoid those altogether. If it looks like you've ordered more than you can chew, feel free to get a take-away bag and eat the extra food later.

It is true that you will get better at potion control with time, but it is important got to get too overconfident. Keep testing your estimate measurement time to time to make sure they are still good.

Important facts to know about Diabetes

People with Diabetes do not need special diet. They should eat
the same stuff that is healthy for everyone- veggies, fruits, whole
grains, and lean meat. They should eat breakfast, lunch, and
dinner. It is important to have multiple small meals in a day and
not have a few big ones as big means can cause the sugar level to
spike, and that is never good for diabetics.

People with diabetes can eat sugar, but not too much of it. Sugar
is just another carbohydrate for the body. However, an excess of
sugar, or any other carbohydrate for that matter, can be harmful.
Sugar is, however, the fastest digesting carbohydrate and spikes
the blood sugar more than the slower digesting carbs. Remember-
the simpler the carbohydrate, the faster it will digest, and the
more spike it will cause in your blood sugar. The more complex
the carb, the slower it will digest, and will give a more sustained
flow of sugar to the blood. Oats are considered good for the body
because they are very complex, and take time to digest, and not
cause a spike in blood sugar. Having said that, as long as the
amount of sugar you're ingesting fits your allowed limit in your
diet plan, it's all good.

**There are many sugar substitutes available naturally, but treat
them as you would treat sugar.** Honey, agave nectar, maple
syrup, brown sugar, and white sugar all contain approximately the
same amount of calories and have an identical effect on your
blood glucose levels. All of these sweeteners are a source of
simple carbohydrates and, like any sugar, will raise blood glucose
quickly.

That does not mean that these are completely off-limits for
diabetics. In moderation, within the bounds of your diet plan,
these can be incorporated into your diet. It is important to know

the calorie content of these sugars, though, so Ill mention these below:

- 1 tablespoon honey = approximately 64 calories, 17 grams of carbohydrate
- 1 tablespoon brown sugar = approximately 52 calories, 13 grams of carbohydrate
- 1 tablespoon white sugar = approximately 48 calories, 13 grams of carbohydrate
- 1 tablespoon agave nectar = approximately 45 calories, 12 grams of carbohydrate
- 1 tablespoon maple syrup = approximately 52 calories, 13 grams of carbohydrate
- 1 packet of artificial sweetener = approximately 4 calories, <1 gram of carbohydrate

Artificial sweeteners are a low-calorie, low-carb options, and they actually work. There are plenty of options available out there in the market right now. Before using one, make sure you consult your dietician or doctor.

Different diabetics have different needs. On an average, approximately 45-60 grams of carbs per meal is the standard. However, this amount can vary depending on your body weight, age, and gender. Talk to your health care expert/doctor to get an idea of how much is ok for you.

Fruits are good, but also a source of sugar. Fruits are great sources of fiber, vitamins, and minerals. Fresh fruits without added sugar are the best option. Canned and frozen fruit without any added sugar are good options too. It is easy to find how much calories and carbs each fruit contains on the internet. Make sure you do, and feel free to incorporate fruits you love into your diet plan as long as they fit your nutritional constraints. I will provide some nutritional info about the most common fruits out there.

The following portions have approximately 15 grams of carbohydrates:

- 1 small piece of whole fruit such as a small apple, small orange, or kiwifruit
- ½ cup of frozen or canned fruit
- ¾–1 cup of fresh berries or melon
- ⅓–½ cup 100% no-sugar-added fruit juice
- 2 tablespoons of dried fruit

Protein is important, and meat isn't the only source.
When looking for sources of protein, look for ones that are low in saturated and trans fats. I'll mention the best lean sources of protein below:

- Eggs, egg whites, and egg substitutes
- Vegetarian proteins: beans, soy products, veggie burgers, nuts, and seeds
- Low-fat or non-fat dairy products
- Fish and shellfish
- Poultry without the skin
- Cheeses with 3 grams of fat or less per ounce
- When you do eat meat, choose lean cuts

It is also possible for diabetics to follow a vegan or vegetarian diet, and still get enough protein. Animal products are great, and rich in essential amino acids, which most plant sources lack. If you can, try to incorporate at least some animal products in your diet. However, it not completely necessary, just a little more convenient. You can easily rely on plant sources to get your daily requirement of protein. Make sure you eat plenty of soy products, vegetables, fruits, beans, and whole grains.

Whole grains are better than refined grains, but all grains are carbohydrates. Whole grains contain more fiber, vitamins, and minerals as compared to their refined counterparts, but are still comprised primarily of carbohydrates, and you should watch how much you eat if you're diabetic. That being said, even diabetics do need some carbohydrates in their diet, and these foods are a good option. Just watch your potion sizes.

Diabetics can eat potatoes and sweet potatoes. Starchy vegetables are highly nutritious sources of carbohydrates, and are loaded with potassium, fiber, and vitamin C. As is the case with every other source of carbohydrates, you will need to watch your potion sizes. If you are carb counting, remember that there are approximately 15 grams of carbohydrates in:

- ½ cup of mashed potatoes
- ½ cup of boiled potatoes
- ¼ of a large baked potato with the skin

Food can taste great without salt and fat. When trying to eat healthy, you should keep your salt and fat intake to a minimum. However, that does tend to make the food taste a little bland. Luckily, there are herbs (fresh or dries) and spices to bring the flavour back up! Make a trip to your local grocery store and pick up salt-free spice blends to try on your food! A few of my favorite ways to make bland good taste good without adding salt and fat are:

- Squeezing lemon or lime juice on vegetables, fish, rice, or pasta
- Using onion and garlic to flavor dishes
- Baking meats with sugar-free barbecue sauce or any low-fat marinade
- Adding low-fat, low-calorie condiments, such as mustard, salsa, balsamic vinegar, or hot sauce

Gluten is absolutely safe to eat if you're not gluten intolerant. About one on ten people suffering from diabetes are allergic to gluten. If you're one of the 9 people, you are in luck! Following a gluten free diet can be a pain, and makes meal planning harder. For example, Gluten-free bread can have twice as many grams of carbs as whole wheat bread of the same weight.

Tips for Using Your Slow Cooker

As a kid with a working mom, I was practically brought up on slow cooked food. I'm not complaining, I probably had the most delicious childhood in the whole world. I loved my mom's recipes, and the Crockpot will always have a special spot in my heart. All slow cooker recipes have one thing on their side: TIME!! Normally cooked foods cannot compare to slow cooked foods when it comes to flavor and texture.

Before we get started with the recipes, I would like you to give you a few tips about the Crockpot. Following these will make sure you get optimum results with each recipe.

Now, If you don't already have a slow cooker with you, it is never to late to buy one. Trust me, it is one of the best investments you can make. Depending on the size of your family, the size of the slow cooker you will need will vary.

- For 2–3 person household 3–5-quart slow cooker
- For 4–5 person household 5–6-quart slow cooker
- For a 6+ person household 6½–7-quart slow cooker

Large slow cooker advantages/disadvantages:

Advantages:

- You can fit a loaf pan or a baking dish into a 6- or 7-quart, depending on the shape of your cooker. That enables you to make bread or cakes, or even smaller quantities of main dishes.
- You can feed large groups of people, or make larger quantities of food, allowing for leftovers, or meals, to freeze.

Disadvantages:

- They occupy more storage room.
- They don't fit as easily into a dishwasher.
- If your Crock isn't at least ⅔–¾ full, there's a risk you may burn your food.

Small slow cooker advantages/disadvantages:

Advantages:

- They're great for lots of appetizers, for serving hot drinks, for baking cakes straight in the Crock, and for dorm rooms or apartments.
- Great option for making recipes of smaller quantities.

Disadvantages:

- Food in smaller quantities tends to cook more quickly than larger amounts. So keep an eye on it. Chances are, you won't have many leftovers. So, if you like to have leftovers, a smaller slow cooker may not be a good option for you.

Manual Vs Automatic Slow Cookers: Usually it takes a dish to cook about 6-8 hours in a slow cooker. The thing about automatic slow cookers is that you can set a timer on them and they will turn to warm once the cooking time is done. If you're a working person who stays out for more than the cooking time, it would be better to get an automatic one. If you stay at home, or will cook overnight, a manual slow cooker will do just fine.

Useful Crockpot Tips

- The Meat Thermometer can be a valuable ally when cooking meat. All the chicken recipes will be completely cooked when the meat thermometer shows a reading of around 170 degrees, assuming the thermometer is in the right place.
- Fill your slow cooker between 50% and 75% for best results. Any more than 75% or less than 50% will not produce optimal results.
- If you run a tight ship, you can always prepare ahead of time. Just fill the slow cooker up and keep it in the refrigerator overnight. In the morning, you can either bring the slow cooker to room temperature and cook, or simple cook from the refrigerated state.
- Make sure all the ingredients are cut uniformly so that the cooking is uniform too.
- Slow cookers use little energy, and it's OK to keep them on for long periods of time, like when u sleep or work.
- Slow cookers don't allow evaporation, and hence, it's OK if the contents of the slow cooker seem a little dry.
- It's a good idea to not place the meat directly into the Crockpot. A bed of vegetables always helps, as it adds to the flavor and helps keep the meat moist. You don't have to eat the vegetables, don't worry. Onions, carrots and mushrooms serve this purpose well.
- DO NOT LIFT THE LID WHILE THE FOOD IS COOKING!!!! It lowers the temperature and pressure of the slow cooker and elongates cooking time, and reduces efficiency.
- Almost all slow cookers have a temperature of 200 degree F on the Low setting, and 300 degrees F on High Setting.
- Low setting takes almost double the time to cook the same food as compared to the High setting.

- If the meat is in frozen state, thaw it before you start cooking it.
- Whole chicken takes very long to cook as it has very low surface area. It's best to have it in medium size or small size pieces.
- If the cut of meat is large, it's a good idea to brown it in a skillet before slow cooking it.
- Avoid sudden temperature changes to your slow cooker.

Diabetic Breakfasts and Brunches

Breakfast is the most important meal of the day, and that is especially true for diabetics. If you skip breakfast, you tend to have a big meal later in the day, which can lead to a sudden spike in blood sugar levels. Moreover, there should never be a reason to skip breakfast, considering how delicious breakfast recipes are. Don't believe me? Try out the recipes that follow, and then we'll talk!

All-Bran Date Muffins

Yield: 16 servings, 1 muffin per serving
Preparation Time: 20 minutes
Standing Time: 20 minutes
Baking Time: 20–25 minutes
Ingredients:

- ¾ cup brown sugar
- 1 cup All-Bran cereal
- 1 cup boiling water
- 1 cup chopped dates
- 1 cup chopped nuts
- 1 cup flour
- 1 egg, thoroughly beaten
- 1 Tbsp. vegetable shortening
- 1 tsp. baking powder
- 1 tsp. baking soda

Directions:

1. Mix dates, nuts, baking soda, and shortening. Pour boiling water over mixture and let cool, 20 minutes.
2. Put in sugar, egg, flour, All-Bran, and baking powder. Fold together until blended. Do not use mixer.
3. Spoon batter into thoroughly -oil-coated muffin tins.
4. Bake at 350°F for 20–25 minutes.

Exchange List Value:

- Carbohydrate 1.5
- Fat 1.0

Basic Nutritional Values:

- Calories 150 (Calories from Fat 55)
- Total Fat 6 gm (Saturated Fat 0.8 gm, Trans Fat 0.0 gm, Polyunsaturated Fat 4.0 gm, Monounsaturated Fat 1.1 gm)
- Cholesterol 10 mg
- Sodium 120 mg
- Potassium 160 gm
- Total Carb 24 gm
- Dietary Fiber 3 gm
- Sugars 14 gm
- Protein 3 gm
- Phosphorus 120 gm

Apple Breakfast Risotto

Yield: 4 servings
Preparation Time: 10 minutes
Cooking Time: 8 hours
Preferred Crock-Pot Size: 3-qt.
Ingredients:

- 4 Granny Smith apples, peeled, cored and sliced
- 2 cups no-added-sugar apple juice
- 2 cups water
- 2½ cups arborio rice
- ¼ cup brown sugar
- 1½ tsp. cinnamon
- ¼ tsp. salt
- 1 tsp. vanilla extract
- ⅛ tsp. cloves
- ⅛ tsp. nutmeg
- ¼ cup butter, sliced

Directions:

1. THrow all ingredients into the Crock and stir.
2. Cover and cook on Low for approximately 8 hours.

Exchange List Value:

- Bread/Starch 3.0
- Fruit 2.0
- Fat 1.0

Basic Nutritional Values:

- Calories 221 (Calories from Fat 54)

- Total Fat 6 gm (Saturated Fat 3.6 gm, Trans Fat 0.2 gm, Polyunsaturated Fat 0.27 gm, Monounsaturated Fat 1.7 gm)
- Cholesterol 15 mg
- Sodium 64 mg
- Potassium 153 gm
- Total Carb 69 gm
- Dietary Fiber 3.7 gm
- Sugars 19.6gm
- Protein 16.7 gm
- Phosphorus 4 gm

Apple Oatmeal

Yield: 5 servings
Preparation Time: 20 minutes
Cooking Time: 5–6 hours
Preferred Crock-Pot Size: 3-qt.
Ingredients:

- ¼ tsp. salt
- ½ cup chopped walnuts
- ½ tsp. cinnamon
- 1 cup chopped apples
- 1 cup dry rolled oats
- 1 Tbsp. brown sugar substitute to equal ½ Tbsp. sugar
- 1 Tbsp. honey
- 1 Tbsp. light, soft tub margarine
- 2 cups fat-free milk

Directions:

1. Combine together all ingredients in greased Crock Pot.
2. Cover. Cook on Low for approximately 5–6 hours.
3. Serve with milk or ice cream.

Exchange List Value:

- Carbohydrate 2.0
- Fat 1.5

Basic Nutritional Values:

- Calories 220 (Calories from Fat 89)
- Total Fat 10 gm (Saturated Fat 1.1 gm, Polyunsaturated Fat 6.3 gm, Monounsaturated Fat 1.9 gm)
- Cholesterol 2 mg

- Sodium 180 mg
- Total Carb 28 gm
- Dietary Fiber 3 gm
- Sugars 15 gm
- Protein 8 gm

B & B Blueberry Coffee Cake

Yield: 18 servings, 2x3-inch rectangle per serving
Preparation Time: 15–20 minutes
Baking Time: 55–65 minutes
Ingredients:

- ¾ cup Splenda Sugar Blend
- 1 tsp. salt
- 1½ cups fat-free milk
- 2 eggs
- 4 cups flour
- 4 cups fresh, or frozen, blueberries
- 5 tsp. baking powder
- 6 Tbsp. trans-fat-free tub margarine

Topping:

- ½ tsp. nutmeg
- ⅔ cup flour
- 1 tsp. cinnamon
- 2 Tbsp. Splenda Sugar Blend
- 6 Tbsp. trans-fat-free tub margarine

Directions:

1. In an electric-mixer vessel, combine flour, sweetener, baking powder, salt, margarine, milk, and eggs. Using mixer, whisk vigorously for 30 seconds.
2. If using frozen blueberries, place in big vessel and stir in 3 Tbsp. flour until each blueberry is thoroughly coated. (If using fresh berries, no need to add flour.)
3. Cautiously fold blueberries into batter.
4. Pour into slightly oil-coated 9x13-inch baking pan.

5. For topping, mix sweetener, flour, cinnamon, and nutmeg in a vessel.
6. Using a pastry cutter, or two forks, cut in margarine until small crumbs are attained.
7. Drizzle crumbs uniformly over batter.
8. Bake at 350°F for 55–65 minutes, or until toothpick injected in center of cake comes out unsoiled.

Exchange List Value:

- Starch 1.5
- Carbohydrate 1.0
- Fat 1.0

Basic Nutritional Values:

- Calories 240 (Calories from Fat 55)
- Total Fat 6 gm (Saturated Fat 1.5 gm, Trans Fat 0.0 gm, Polyunsaturated Fat 2.6 gm, Monounsaturated Fat 2.1 gm)
- Cholesterol 20 mg
- Sodium 305 mg
- Potassium 105 gm
- Total Carb 40 gm
- Dietary Fiber 2 gm
- Sugars 14 gm
- Protein 5 gm
- Phosphorus 200 gm

Bacon Cheese Squares

Yield: 12 servings, 3-inch square per serving
Preparation Time: approximately half an hour
Baking Time: 18–24 minutes
Ingredients:

- ½ cup cold water
- ½ cup fat-free milk
- ½ lb. 50–70% reduced-fat turkey bacon, sliced, cooked crisp, and crumbled
- ½ tsp. onion powder
- ¾ cup egg substitute
- 2 cups reduced-fat buttermilk baking mix
- 3 eggs
- 4 oz. 75%-reduced-fat cheese, sliced

Directions:

1. In a vessel, mix the baking mix and water. Stir 20 strokes.
2. Turn onto a floured surface. Knead 10 times.
3. Roll into a 10x14-inch rectangle. Fold into quarters (without pressing down on the folds) and lay on the bottom and halfway up the sides of a oil-coated 9x13-inch baking dish.
4. Lay cheese uniformly over dough. Drizzle with bacon.
5. In the mixing vessel, whisk together eggs, egg substitute, milk, and onion powder.
6. Pour egg-milk mixture on the bacon.
7. Bake at 425°F for 18–20 minutes, or until a knife blade injected in center comes out unsoiled. If it doesn't, continue baking another 4 minutes. Test again. Keep on baking if needed, or remove from oven.
8. Letstand 10 minutes before cutting into squares and serving.

Exchange List Value:

- Starch 1.0
- Lean Meat 1.0
- Fat 0.5

Basic Nutritional Values:

- Calories 140 (Calories from Fat 45)
- Total Fat 5 gm (Saturated Fat 1.5 gm, Trans Fat 0.0 gm, Polyunsaturated Fat 0.9 gm, Monounsaturated Fat 2.0 gm)
- Cholesterol 60 mg
- Sodium 440 mg
- Potassium 110 gm
- Total Carb 15 gm
- Dietary Fiber 1 gm
- Sugars 2 gm
- Protein 9 gm
- Phosphorus 215 gm

Baked Eggs

Make 8 servings, 2¾×3½-inch rectangle per serving
Preparation Time: 15 minutes
Baking Time: 40–45 minutes
Ingredients:

- ½ cup grated reduced-fat cheddar cheese
- 1 cup fat-free milk
- 1 cup reduced-fat buttermilk baking mix
- 1 egg, sslightly beaten
- 1 tsp. dried parsley
- 1¼ cups egg substitute
- 1½ cups fat-free cottage cheese
- 2 Tbsp. trans-fat-free tub margarine
- 2 tsp. chopped onion

Directions:

1. Chop margarine into chunks and put in 7x11-inch baking dish. Turn oven to 350°F and put dish in oven to melt margarine.
2. In the meantime, combine buttermilk baking mix, cottage cheese, onion, parsley, cheese, egg, egg substitute, and milk in big mixing vessel.
3. Pour mixture over melted margarine. Stir slightly to spread margarine.
4. Bake 40–45 minutes until firm but not drying out.
5. Letstand 10 minutes. Chop in rectangles and serve.

Exchange List Value:

- Carbohydrate 1.0
- Lean Meat 2.0

Basic Nutritional Values:

- Calories 155 (Calories from Fat 45)
- Total Fat 5 gm (Saturated Fat 1.5 gm, Trans Fat 0.0 gm, Polyunsaturated Fat 1.2 gm, Monounsaturated Fat 1.8 gm)
- Cholesterol 30 mg
- Sodium 460 mg
- Potassium 195 gm
- Total Carb 15 gm
- Dietary Fiber 0 gm
- Sugars 4 gm
- Protein 12 gm
- Phosphorus 250 gm

Baked French Toast with Cream Cheese

Yield: 10 servings
Preparation Time: 15–20 minutes
Baking Time: 40–45 minutes
Ingredients:

- ¼ cup maple syrup, or pancake syrup
- ¼ cup trans-fat-free tub margarine
- ½ cup fat-free half-and-half
- 10 eggs
- 1-lb. loaf firm bread, divided (Preferably one day old)
- 2 cup berries of your choice—strawberries, blueberries, or raspberries
- 8-oz. pkg. fat-free cream cheese

Directions:

1. Cut the bread into cubes and layer half in thoroughly -oil-coated 9x13-inch baking pan.
2. Chop cream cheese into small pieces and scatter across bread.
3. Drizzle with berries.
4. Cover berries with left over half of bread.
5. In mixing vessel, whisk together eggs, half-and-half, syrup, and melted margarine.
6. Pour what is inside the baking pan over bread.
7. Apply pressure until bread is submerged to the maximum.
8. Cover and place in the refrigerator for 8 hours, or overnight.
9. Bake with an open lid at 375°F for 40–45 minutes, or until slightly browned and puffy.

Exchange List Value:

- Starch 1.5
- Carbohydrate 0.5
- Lean Meat 2.0
- Fat 0.5

Basic Nutritional Values:

- Calories 270 (Calories from Fat 70)
- Total Fat 8 gm (Saturated Fat 2.4 gm, Trans Fat 0.0 gm, Polyunsaturated Fat 2.4 gm, Monounsaturated Fat 3.0 gm)
- Cholesterol 190 mg
- Sodium 485 mg
- Potassium 245 gm
- Total Carb 33 gm
- Dietary Fiber 1 gm
- Sugars 9 gm
- Protein 13 gm
- Phosphorus 285 gm

Baked Oatmeal

Yield: 12 servings, 3-inch square per serving
Preparation Time: 10 minutes
Baking Time: 20–25 minutes
Ingredients:

- ½ cup raisins or dried cranberries
- 1 cup fat-free milk
- 1 tsp. salt
- 2 eggs, lightly beaten
- 2 Tbsp. trans-fat-free tub margarine, melted
- 2 tsp. baking powder
- 3 cups quick oatmeal
- 3 Tbsp. Splenda Brown Sugar Blend

Directions:

1. Mix brown sugar blend, margarine, and eggs in mixing vessel.
2. Combine oatmeal, baking powder, milk, and salt and add to vessel. Stir in raisins or cranberries.
3. Pour into 9x13-inch baking pan.
4. Bake at 350°F for approximately 20–25 minutes.

Exchange List Value:

- Starch 1.0
- Fruit 0.5
- Fat 0.5

Basic Nutritional Values:

- Calories 140 (Calories from Fat 30)

- Total Fat 4 gm (Saturated Fat 0.8 gm, Trans Fat 0.0 gm, Polyunsaturated Fat 1.2 gm, Monounsaturated Fat 1.2 gm)
- Cholesterol 30 mg
- Sodium 290 mg
- Potassium 165 gm
- Total Carb 23 gm
- Dietary Fiber 2 gm
- Sugars 6 gm
- Protein 5 gm
- Phosphorus 205 gm

Banana Chocolate Chip Muffins

Yield: 24 servings, 1 muffin per serving
Preparation Time: 15 minutes
Baking Time: 12–18 minutes
Ingredients:

- ½ cup chocolate chips
- 1 egg
- 1 tsp. baking powder
- 1 tsp. baking soda
- 1½ cups flour
- 4 big ripe bananas, mashed
- 5⅓ Tbsp. trans-fat-free tub margarine, melted
- 6 Tbsp. Splenda Sugar Blend

Directions:

1. In a mixing vessel of decent size, mix together bananas, Splenda, egg, and flour.
2. Combine in baking soda, baking powder, and melted margarine.
3. Stir in chocolate chips.
4. Bake in lined muffin tins at 375°F for 12–18 minutes, or until toothpick injected in center comes out unsoiled. Check after 12 minutes to protect muffins from getting overbaked.

Exchange List Value:

- Carbohydrate 1.0
- Fat 0.5

Basic Nutritional Values:

- Calories 100 (Calories from Fat 25)
- Total Fat 3 gm (Saturated Fat 1.2 gm, Trans Fat 0.0 gm, Polyunsaturated Fat 0.9 gm, Monounsaturated Fat 1.1 gm)
- Cholesterol 10 mg
- Sodium 90 mg
- Potassium 105 gm
- Total Carb 17 gm
- Dietary Fiber 1 gm
- Sugars 8 gm
- Protein 1 gm
- Phosphorus 40 gm

Berry Oatmeal

Yield: 2–3 servings
Preparation Time: 5 minutes
Cooking Time: 7 hours
Preferred Crock-Pot Size: 2-qt.
Ingredients:

- ½ cup steel-cut oats
- ½ tsp. vanilla extract
- 1 cup combined berries of your choice (if frozen, defrost first and drain juice)
- 2 cups unsweetened vanilla almond milk

Directions:

1. Coat the slow coooker with nonstick spray.
2. Throw all ingredients into Crock and stir gently.
3. Cover and cook on Low for approximately 7 hours.

Exchange List Value:

- Bread/Starch 1.0
- Fruit 1.0
- Milk 0.5
- Fat 1.0

Basic Nutritional Values:

- Calories 193 (Calories from Fat 36)

- Total Fat 4 gm (Saturated Fat 0.2 gm, Trans Fat 0 gm, Polyunsaturated Fat 1.1 gm, Monounsaturated Fat 1.9 gm)
- Cholesterol 0 mg
- Sodium 153 mg

- Potassium 304 gm
- Total Carb 35 gm
- Dietary Fiber 4 gm
- Sugars 19gm
- Protein 4 gm
- Phosphorus 119 gm

Blueberry French Toast

Yield: 12 servings
Preparation Time: approximately half an hour
Chilling Time: 6–8 hours or overnight
Baking Time: 60 minutes
Ingredients:

- ⅓ cup honey
- 1 cup frozen blueberries
- 1½ cups egg substitute
- 12 slices day-old bread
- 2 cups fat-free milk
- 4 oz. cream cheese
- 4 oz. Neufchâtel (⅓-less-fat) cream cheese
- 6 eggs

Sauce:

- ¼ cup Splenda Sugar Blend
- 1 cup blueberries
- 1 cup water
- 2 Tbsp. cornstarch

Directions:

1. Oil-coat 9x13-inch baking pan.
2. Cut the bread into cubes and spread in pan.
3. Cube cream cheese. Distribute uniformly over bread.
4. Drizzle blueberries on top.
5. In a mixing vessel, mix eggs, egg substitute, milk, and honey.
6. Pour over baking-pan contents.
7. Cover. Refrigerate 6–8 hours, or overnight.

8. Take out from refrigerator approximately half an hour before baking.
9. Bake, covered, at 350°F for approximately half an hour.
10. Uncover. Bake for another half hour. Serve with sauce.
11. Make Sauce: Combine Splenda, cornstarch, and water in a saucepan. Bring to a boil.
12. Combine in blueberries.
13. Lower heat, cooking until blueberries burst.
14. Serve warm over French toast.

Exchange List Value:

- Starch 1.0
- Carbohydrate 1.0
- Lean Meat 1.0
- Fat 0.5

Basic Nutritional Values:

- Calories 225 (Calories from Fat 55)
- Total Fat 6 gm (Saturated Fat 2.2 gm, Trans Fat 0.0 gm, Polyunsaturated Fat 1.0 gm, Monounsaturated Fat 1.7 gm)
- Cholesterol 100 mg
- Sodium 380 mg
- Potassium 230 gm
- Total Carb 32 gm
- Dietary Fiber 1 gm
- Sugars 18 gm
- Protein 12 gm
- Phosphorus 185 gm

Breakfast Apple Cobbler

Yield: 8 servings
Preparation Time: 25 minutes
Cooking Time: 2–9 hours
Preferred Crock-Pot Size: 4- or 5-qt.
Ingredients:

- 2 cups granola
- 2 Tbsp. light, soft tub margarine, melted
- 2 Tbsp. sugar substitute to equal 1 Tbsp. sugar
- 8 moderate apples, cored, peeled, sliced
- dash cinnamon
- juice of 1 lemon

Directions:

1. Mix ingredients in Crock Pot.
2. Cover. Cook on Low 7–9 hours, or on High 2–3 hours

Exchange List Value:

- Starch 1.5
- Fruit 1.5
- Fat 1.0

Basic Nutritional Values:

- Calories 221 (Calories from Fat 57)
- Total Fat 6 gm (Saturated Fat 2.1 gm, Polyunsaturated Fat 1.9 gm, Monounsaturated Fat 1.7 gm)
- Cholesterol 0 mg
- Sodium 102 mg
- Total Carb 42 gm
- Dietary Fiber 4 gm

- Sugars 29 gm
- Protein 2 gm

Breakfast Pie

Yield: 6 servings
Preparation Time: 20 minutes
Baking Time: 30 minutes
Ingredients:

- ½ cup reduced-fat buttermilk baking mix
- 1 cup 75%-less-fat shredded cheddar cheese
- 1 cup chopped bell pepper, red or green
- 1 cup chopped onion
- 1 cup fat-free milk
- 2 eggs
- 8 oz. lower-sodium ham

Directions:

1. Brown ham, onion, and bell pepper in frying pan on stove until done. Drain off drippings.
2. Put cooked ingredients in a oil-coated 9-inch pie plate.
3. Top with coat of shredded cheese.
4. In a mixing vessel, whisk baking mix, milk, and eggs together. Pour over ingredients in pie plate.
5. Bake at 400°F for approximately half an hour.
6. Letstand 5–10 minutes before cutting and serving.

Exchange List Value:

- Carbohydrate 1.0
- Lean Meat 2.0

Basic Nutritional Values:

- Calories 170 (Calories from Fat 40)

- Total Fat 4.5 gm (Saturated Fat 1.8 gm, Trans Fat 0.0 gm, Polyunsaturated Fat 0.6 gm, Monounsaturated Fat 1.7 gm)
- Cholesterol 85 mg
- Sodium 595 mg
- Potassium 295 gm
- Total Carb 15 gm
- Dietary Fiber 1 gm
- Sugars 6 gm
- Protein 17 gm
- Phosphorus 310 gm

Breakfast Soufflé

Yield: 12 servings, 3-inch square per serving
Preparation Time: 20 minutes
Standing Time: 12 hours or overnight
Baking Time: 1 hour
Ingredients:

- ½ lb. reduced-fat pork sausage
- ¾ cup grated 75%-less-fat cheddar cheese
- ¾ tsp. salt
- 1½ tsp. dry mustard
- 2¼ cups egg substitute
- 3 cups fat-free milk
- 3 slices bread, cubed

Directions:

1. Brown pork sausage and drain surplus fat. Set aside.
2. Mix egg substitute, milk, mustard, and salt. Add sausage, bread, and cheese.
3. Ladle into oil-coated 9x13-inch pan. Cover and place in the refrigerator overnight.
4. Bake, with an open lid, at 350°F for 60 minutes.

Exchange List Value:

- Carbohydrate 0.5
- Lean Meat 2.0

Basic Nutritional Values:

- Calories 115 (Calories from Fat 35)
- Total Fat 4 gm (Saturated Fat 1.4 gm, Trans Fat 0.0 gm, Polyunsaturated Fat 0.5 gm, Monounsaturated Fat 1.5 gm)

- Cholesterol 15 mg
- Sodium 440 mg
- Potassium 220 gm
- Total Carb 7 gm
- Dietary Fiber 0 gm
- Sugars 4 gm
- Protein 12 gm
- Phosphorus 135 gm

Brunch Delight

Yield: 12 servings, 3-inch square per serving
Preparation Time: 15 minutes
Baking Time: 35–45 minutes
Ingredients:

- ¼ tsp. salt
- ½ cup chopped green bell pepper
- ½ cup chopped onion
- ½ lb. extra-lean 95%-fat-free cooked ham, cut into small cubes
- ½ tsp. dill weed
- ½ tsp. pepper
- 1 cup milk
- 1 cup shredded 75%-less-fat cheddar cheese
- 16 oz. frozen shredded hash brown potatoes, thawed
- 2 cups egg substitute
- 4 eggs

Directions:

1. Fry onion and green pepper in small nonstick frying pan. Or cook just until soft in microwave.
2. In big vessel whisk together eggs, egg substitute, and milk.
3. Combine in cooked vegetables, ham, potatoes, cheese, salt, pepper, and dill weed.
4. Spoon into thoroughly-oil-coated 9x13-inch baking pan.
5. Bake at 350°F for approximately 35–45 minutes, or until knife blade injected in center comes out unsoiled.
6. Letstand 10 minutes before cutting into squares to serve.

Exchange List Value:

- Starch 0.5

- Lean Meat 2.0

Basic Nutritional Values:

- Calories 135 (Calories from Fat 30)
- Total Fat 4 gm (Saturated Fat 1.4 gm, Trans Fat 0.0 gm, Polyunsaturated Fat 0.5 gm, Monounsaturated Fat 1.3 gm)
- Cholesterol 75 mg
- Sodium 460 mg
- Potassium 335 gm
- Total Carb 10 gm
- Dietary Fiber 1 gm
- Sugars 2 gm
- Protein 15 gm
- Phosphorus 160 gm

Brunch Enchiladas

Yield: 16 servings, 1 filled tortilla per serving
Preparation Time: 20–35 minutes
Chilling Time: 8 hours, or overnight
Baking Time: 45–60 minutes
Standing Time: 5–10 minutes
Ingredients:

- ½ tsp. pepper
- ¾ cup chopped bell peppers
- ¾ cup chopped onion
- 1 Tbsp. canola oil
- 1½ cups fat-free milk
- 1½ cups shredded 75%-less-fat cheese, divided
- 16 6-inch flour tortillas
- 2 cups egg substitute
- 2 cups extra-lean chopped cooked ham
- 2 Tbsp. flour
- 3 moderate tomatoes, sliced
- 8 eggs
- 8-oz. container fat-free sour cream, divided

Directions:

1. In saucepan, fry peppers and onion in oil until soft.
2. Combine in meat and cook until heated completely.
3. Distribute 1 Tbsp. of sour cream in a strip through the center of each tortilla.
4. Ladle 2 Tbsp. meat mixture on top of sour cream on each tortilla.
5. Top with ½ Tbsp. cheese on each tortilla. (Save 1 cup cheese for topping enchiladas after baking.)
6. Roll up and lay seams-down in two thoroughly -oil-coated 9x13-inch baking pans.

7. In a big mixing vessel, whisk together egg substitute, eggs, milk, flour, and pepper.
8. PLace over tortillas. Cover and place in the refrigerator overnight.
9. Take out from refrigerator for approximately half an hour before baking.
10. Bake with an open lid at 350°F for 45–60 minutes, or until heated through.
11. Take out from oven. Top with tomato slices.
12. Allow to stand 5–10 minutes before serving.

Exchange List Value:

- Starch 1.0
- Carbohydrate 0.5
- Lean Meat 2.0
- Fat 0.5

Basic Nutritional Values:

- Calories 230 (Calories from Fat 70)
- Total Fat 8 gm (Saturated Fat 2.4 gm, Trans Fat 0.0 gm, Polyunsaturated Fat 1.3 gm, Monounsaturated Fat 3.3 gm)
- Cholesterol 110 mg
- Sodium 595 mg
- Potassium 330 gm
- Total Carb 23 gm
- Dietary Fiber 2 gm
- Sugars 4 gm
- Protein 17 gm
- Phosphorus 225 gm

Brunch Pizza

Yield: 8 servings, 3¼×4½-inch rectangle per serving
Preparation Time: 60 minutes
Baking Time: 15–18 minutes
Ingredients:

- ¼ tsp. Italian seasoning
- ⅓ cup fat-free sour cream
- ½ lb. fresh mushrooms, sliced
- ¾ cup shredded 75%-reduced-fat cheddar cheese
- 1 clove garlic, minced
- 1 small green bell pepper, finely chopped
- 1 small onion, finely chopped
- 1 Tbsp. canola oil, divided
- 2 cups egg substitute
- 2 plum tomatoes, sliced thin
- 2 Tbsp. chopped bacon
- 3 oz. fat-free cream cheese, softened to room temperature
- 8-oz. pkg. reduced-fat crescent rolls
- salsa and additional sour cream, optional

Directions:

1. Open crescent dough tube and unroll. Push crescent dough over bottom and partway up sides of 9x13-inch baking pan.
2. Bake at 375°F for 6–8 minutes.
3. In the meantime, cook bacon in big frying pan until crispy. Take out bacon and let drain on a paper towel.
4. Fry mushrooms, onions, and pepper in ½ Tbsp. oil until just tender.
5. Take out vegetables from pan and set aside.

6. Heat other ½ Tbsp. oil in frying pan. Add egg substitute and cook, stirring, until almost set.
7. In a mixing vessel, whisk together cream cheese, sour cream, garlic, and Italian seasoning. Spread over crescent-dough crust in baking pan.
8. Top with egg mixture, and then meat, and then fried vegetables.
9. Crown with tomato slices and then cheese.
10. Bake at 375°F for approximately 15–18 minutes, or until cheese is liquified.
11. Serve with salsa and extra sour cream, if you wish, for each person to add as they want.

Exchange List Value:

- Starch 1.0
- Vegetable 1.0
- Lean Meat 2.0
- Fat 0.5

Basic Nutritional Values:

- Calories 200 (Calories from Fat 70)
- Total Fat 8 gm (Saturated Fat 2.5 gm, Trans Fat 0.0 gm, Polyunsaturated Fat 1.6 gm, Monounsaturated Fat 1.9 gm)
- Cholesterol 5 mg
- Sodium 555 mg
- Potassium 380 gm
- Total Carb 19 gm
- Dietary Fiber 1 gm
- Sugars 6 gm
- Protein 15 gm
- Phosphorus 270 gm

California Egg Bake

Yield: 2 servings
Preparation Time: 10–15 minutes
Baking Time: 25–30 minutes
Ingredients:

- ⅛ tsp. salt
- ¼ cup fat-free sour cream
- ¼ cup reduced-fat shredded cheddar cheese
- ¾ cup egg substitute
- 1 green onion, sliced
- 1 medium tomato, chopped

Directions:

1. In a small vessel, whisk egg substitute, sour cream, and salt.
2. Combine in the tomato, onion, and cheese.
3. Pour into oil-coated 2-cup baking dish.
4. Bake at 350°F for approximately 25–30 minutes, or until a knife injected in center comes out unsoiled.

Exchange List Value:

- Carbohydrate 0.5
- Lean Meat 2.0

Basic Nutritional Values:

- Calories 125 (Calories from Fat 30)
- Total Fat 4 gm (Saturated Fat 1.9 gm, Trans Fat 0.0 gm, Polyunsaturated Fat 0.2 gm, Monounsaturated Fat 0.7 gm)
- Cholesterol 10 mg

- Sodium 480 mg
- Potassium 350 gm
- Total Carb 10 gm
- Dietary Fiber 1 gm
- Sugars 4 gm
- Protein 14 gm
- Phosphorus 140 gm

Cheese Soufflé Casserole

Yield: 6 servings
Preparation Time: 20 minutes
Cooking Time: 3–4 hours
Preferred Crock-Pot Size: 3- or 4-qt.
Ingredients:

- 1 cup cooked, chopped extra-lean, lower-sodium ham
- 1 cup fat-free evaporated milk
- 1 cup fat-free half-and-half
- 1 Tbsp. parsley
- 2 cups grated fat-free cheddar cheese
- 4 eggs
- 8 slices bread (crusts removed), cubed or torn into squares
- paprika

Directions:

1. Lightly grease Crock Pot. Alternate layers of bread and cheese and ham.
2. Combine together eggs, half-and-half, milk, and parsley. Pour over bread in Crock Pot.
3. Drizzle with paprika.
4. Cover and cook on Low 3–4 hours. The longer cooking time will give you a firmer, dryer dish.
5. Approximately 30 minutes before finish, raise temperature to High and take the lid off.

Exchange List Value:

- Starch 1.0
- Fat-Free Milk 0.5
- Lean Meat 2.0

Basic Nutritional Values:

- Calories 233 (Calories from Fat 46)
- Total Fat 5 gm (Saturated Fat 1.9 gm, Polyunsaturated Fat 0.9 gm, Monounsaturated Fat 1.6 gm)
- Cholesterol 159 mg
- Sodium 650 mg
- Total Carb 22 gm
- Dietary Fiber 0 gm
- Sugars 9 gm
- Protein 23 gm

Cinnamon Rolls—Easy Method

Yield: 12 rolls, 1 roll per serving
Thawing Time: 8 hours or overnight
Preparation Time: 15–20 minutes
Rising Time: 4–5 hours, or overnight
Baking Time: 20–25 minutes
Ingredients:

- 1 lb. loaf frozen bread dough
- 1½ cups granulated Splenda, divided
- 1½ Tbsp. fat-free milk
- 2 tsp. cinnamon
- 2⅔ Tbsp. cornstarch
- 8 Tbsp. trans-fat-free tub margarine

Directions:

1. Thaw dough to room temperature.
2. Oil-coat a 9×13-inch baking pan.
3. In a long, flat dish, combine cinnamon and ½ cup sugar substitute.
4. Melt margarine.
5. Chop thawed bread dough diagonally into 12 pieces.
6. Roll each piece of dough between your hands until a rope like structure is attained.
7. Coat each piece of dough with melted margarine, and then dip in cinnamon-sugar. Use a spoon to cover rope thoroughly with mixture.
8. Tie each buttered-sugared piece in a loose knot. Place in oil-coated 9×13-inch baking pan, keeping maximum between knots to give space for rising.
9. Cover loosely and let set until knots double in size, or place in the refrigerator overnight.

10. Set out in morning and let rise until doubled, if knots haven't risen fully.
11. Bake at 350°F for 20–25 minutes.
12. In the meantime, prepare glaze. Blend residual 1 cup Splenda in blender with cornstarch to a fine powder.
13. Combine the blended sugar and milk together in a vessel until smooth.
14. Drizzle glaze over cooled buns.

Exchange List Value:

- Starch 1.5
- Fat 1.0

Basic Nutritional Values:

- Calories 170 (Calories from Fat 65)
- Total Fat 7 gm (Saturated Fat 1.5 gm, Trans Fat 0.0 gm, Polyunsaturated Fat 2.9 gm, Monounsaturated Fat 2.1 gm)
- Cholesterol 0 mg
- Sodium 280 mg
- Potassium 50 gm
- Total Carb 24 gm
- Dietary Fiber 1 gm
- Sugars 4 gm
- Protein 3 gm
- Phosphorus 45 gm

Country Breakfast Pizza

Yield: 10 servings
Preparation Time: 25–30 minutes
Baking Time: 27 minutes
Ingredients:

- ¼ cup real maple syrup
- ¼ lb. lower-fat bulk pork sausage
- ½ green pepper, diced
- ½ tsp. salt
- ⅔ cup, plus 2 Tbsp., all-purpose flour
- 1 cup shredded 75%-reduced-fat cheddar cheese, divided
- 1 cup whole wheat pastry flour
- 1 Tbsp. flax meal, optional
- 1½ Tbsp. olive oil
- 2 tsp. baking powder
- 2¼ cups egg substitute
- maple syrup, or ketchup, for serving
- scant ½ cup fat-free milk

Directions:

1. Put oil in a 9x13-inch baking dish.
2. In a good-sized vessel, combine flours, flax if you wish, baking powder, and salt.
3. Pour in maple syrup and milk. Stir to combine.
4. Knead a few minutes in vessel, or on countertop, to make a ball.
5. Push dough into oiled pan.
6. Bake 12 minutes at 425°F. Take out from the oven.
7. While crust is baking, brown sausage and pepper in frying pan until pink is gone from meat and pepper is just tender. Stir regularly to break up meat. Place cooked meat and pepper on platter and keep warm. Discard drippings.

8. Beat egg substitute in mixing vessel. Pour into frying pan used for sausage. Stir regularly. Add ⅔ cup cheese while eggs are cooking.
9. When crust is cooked, crown with sausage, then eggs, and then residual cheese.
10. Bake 10 additional minutes or until cheese is molten.
11. Serve instantly with maple syrup or ketchup.

Exchange List Value:

- Starch 1.0
- Carbohydrate 0.5
- Lean Meat 2.0

Basic Nutritional Values:

- Calories 200 (Calories from Fat 45)
- Total Fat 5 gm (Saturated Fat 1.5 gm, Trans Fat 0.0 gm, Polyunsaturated Fat 0.6 gm, Monounsaturated Fat 2.5 gm)
- Cholesterol 10 mg
- Sodium 435 mg
- Potassium 225 gm
- Total Carb 25 gm
- Dietary Fiber 2 gm
- Sugars 6 gm
- Protein 13 gm
- Phosphorus 235 gm

Cranberry Buttermilk Scones

Yield: 16 servings, 1 scone per serving
Preparation Time: 20 minutes
Baking Time: 15–20 minutes
Ingredients:

- ¼ tsp. ground cinnamon
- ½ tsp. baking soda
- ¾ tsp. salt
- 1 cup dried cranberries
- 1 cup fat-free buttermilk
- 1 Tbsp. fat-free milk
- 1 tsp. grated orange peel
- 12 Tbsp. cold trans-fat-free tub margarine
- 2 Tbsp. sugar
- 2½ tsp. baking powder
- 2⅔ Tbsp. Splenda Sugar Blend
- 3 cups flour

Directions:

1. In a vessel, mix flour, Splenda, baking powder, salt, and baking soda.
2. Chop in margarine, using a pastry cutter or two knives, until mixture looks like small peas.
3. Mix in buttermilk, just until blended.
4. Fold in cranberries and orange peel.
5. Turn dough onto floured surface. Separate dough in half.
6. Mould each portion into a sphere. Pat each into a 6-inch circle.
7. Chop each circle into six wedges.
8. Place on slightly oil-coated baking sheet.
9. Brush tops with milk.

10. In a small vessel, mix 2 Tbsp. sugar with cinnamon. Drizzle on top of wedges.
11. Bake at 400°F for approximately 15–20 minutes, or until golden brown.

Exchange List Value:

- Starch 1.5
- Fruit 0.5
- Fat 1.0

Basic Nutritional Values:

- Calories 185 (Calories from Fat 65)
- Total Fat 7 gm (Saturated Fat 1.4 gm, Trans Fat 0.0 gm, Polyunsaturated Fat 2.8 gm, Monounsaturated Fat 2.1 gm)
- Cholesterol 0 mg
- Sodium 290 mg
- Potassium 55 gm
- Total Carb 29 gm
- Dietary Fiber 1 gm
- Sugars 10 gm
- Protein 3 gm
- Phosphorus 115 gm

Creamy Old-Fashioned Oatmeal

Yield: 5 servings
Preparation Time: 5 minutes
Cooking Time: 6 hours
Preferred Crock-Pot Size: 3-qt.
Ingredients:

- 1⅓ cups dry rolled oats
- 2½ cups, plus 1 Tbsp., water
- dash salt

Directions:

1. Combine together cereal, water, and salt in Crock Pot.
2. Cook on Low for approximately 6 hours.

Exchange List Value:

4. Starch 1.0

Basic Nutritional Values:

- Calories 83 (Calories from Fat 12)
- Total Fat 1 gm (Saturated Fat 0.3 gm, Polyunsaturated Fat 0.5 gm, Monounsaturated Fat 0.4 gm)
- Cholesterol 0 mg
- Sodium 1 mg
- Total Carb 14 gm
- Dietary Fiber 2 gm
- Sugars 0 gm
- Protein 3 gm

Easy Quiche

Yield: 6 servings, 1 slice per serving
Preparation Time: 15 minutes
Baking Time: 45–55 minutes
Ingredients:

- ¼ cup chopped mushrooms, optional
- ¼ cup chopped onion
- ¼ tsp. salt
- ½ cup whole wheat flour
- 1 Tbsp. trans-fat-free tub margarine
- 1 tsp. canola oil
- 1½ cups fat-free milk
- 2 Tbsp. bacon bits, chopped ham, or browned sausage
- 3 oz. 75%-less-fat cheddar cheese, shredded
- 4 eggs

Directions:

1. Sauté onion and mushrooms (if using) in oil.
2. Mix cheese, meat, and vegetables in oil-coated 9-inch pie pan.
3. Mix residual ingredients in moderate vessel. Pour over meat and vegetables mixture.
4. Bake at 350°F for approximately 45–55 minutes, or until the center is set. This quiche will make its own crust.

Exchange List Value:

- Carbohydrate 1.0
- Lean Meat 2.0

Basic Nutritional Values:

- Calories 135 (Calories from Fat 35)
- Total Fat 4 gm (Saturated Fat 1.5 gm, Trans Fat 0.0 gm, Polyunsaturated Fat 0.9 gm, Monounsaturated Fat 1.4 gm)
- Cholesterol 10 mg
- Sodium 400 mg
- Potassium 255 gm
- Total Carb 12 gm
- Dietary Fiber 1 gm
- Sugars 4 gm
- Protein 13 gm
- Phosphorus 170 gm

Egg and Broccoli Casserole

Yield: 8 servings
Preparation Time: 20 minutes
Cooking Time: 3½–4 hours
Preferred Crock-Pot Size: 4-qt.
Ingredients:

- ⅓ cup flour
- 10-oz. pkg. frozen chopped broccoli, thawed and drained
- 1½ cups shredded cheddar cheese
- 2 Tbsp. canola oil
- 24-oz. carton small-curd 1% milkfat cottage cheese
- 3 Tbsp. finely chopped onion
- 6 eggs, beaten
- shredded cheese, optional

Directions:

1. Mix first 7 ingredients. Pour into greased Crock Pot.
2. Cover and cook on High 60 minutes. Stir. Reduce heat to Low. Cover and cook 2½–3 hours, or until temperature reaches 160°F and eggs are set.
3. Drizzle with cheese, if using, and serve.

Exchange List Value:

- Carbohydrate 0.5
- Lean Meat 3.0

Basic Nutritional Values:

- Calories 211 (Calories from Fat 74)
- Total Fat 8 gm (Saturated Fat 2.3 gm, Polyunsaturated Fat 1.6 gm, Monounsaturated Fat 3.7 gm)

- Cholesterol 165 mg
- Sodium 550 mg
- Total Carb 10 gm
- Dietary Fiber 1 gm
- Sugars 5 gm
- Protein 23 gm

Egg Casserole

Yield: 6 servings
Preparation Time: 15 minutes
Baking Time: 35–40 minutes
Ingredients:

- ½ cup chopped green onions
- ⅔ cup butter-flavored cracker crumbs (about 16 crackers, crushed)
- 1 cup 75%-less-fat shredded sharp cheddar cheese
- 1 Tbsp. vegetable oil
- 2 cups egg substitute
- 2–3 cloves garlic, minced
- 4- or 6½-oz. jar marinated artichoke hearts
- 4½-oz. can sliced mushrooms, drained

Directions:

1. Drain artichokes. Chop artichokes into small pieces.
2. In small frying pan, fry green onions and garlic in oil until tender.
3. In big vessel, whisk egg substitute.
4. Combine in artichokes, onion mixture, mushrooms, cheese, and cracker crumbs.
5. Bake at 350°F for approximately35–40 minutes.

Exchange List Value:

- Carbohydrate 1.0
- Lean Meat 2.0
- Fat 0.5

Basic Nutritional Values:

- Calories 165 (Calories from Fat 55)
- Total Fat 6 gm (Saturated Fat 1.3 gm, Trans Fat 0.0 gm, Polyunsaturated Fat 2.2 gm, Monounsaturated Fat 2.0 gm)
- Cholesterol 5 mg
- Sodium 480 mg
- Potassium 230 gm
- Total Carb 11 gm
- Dietary Fiber 1 gm
- Sugars 2 gm
- Protein 16 gm
- Phosphorus 150 gm

Egg Scramble

Yield: 6 servings, 4½–5½ oz. per serving
Preparation Time: 30–45 minutes
Cooking Time: 10 minutes
Ingredients:

- ⅛ tsp. pepper
- ¼ cup chopped green bell pepper
- ¼ cup fat-free milk
- ¼ tsp. garlic salt
- ⅓ cup fat-free sour cream
- ½ cup chopped onion
- ½ cup chopped red bell pepper
- ½ cup real bacon bits
- ½ cup shredded 75%-less-fat cheddar, or Cooper sharp, cheese
- ½ tsp. onion salt
- 1 moderate-big potato, enough to make ¾ cup grated potatoes
- 1 cup egg substitute
- 1 Tbsp. canola oil
- 4 eggs

Directions:

1. Place the whole potato with skin on in a small pan. Pour in about ½ inch water, cover, and cook over low heat until fork-tender.
2. Take out and let reach room temperature.
3. Chill completely. Grate.
4. Brown peppers and onion in canola oil 3–5 minutes.
5. In a blender, mix eggs, egg substitute, sour cream, milk, onion salt, garlic salt, and pepper. Cover and process until smooth.

6. Stir grated potato and bacon into vegetables in frying pan.
7. Pour egg mixture on top of the vegetables.
8. Cook and stir over moderate heat until eggs are set.
9. Drizzle with cheese. Cover frying pan with lid until cheese melts.
10. Chop in wedges in frying pan and serve on heated dinner plates.

Exchange List Value:

- Carbohydrate 1.0
- Lean Meat 2.0
- Fat 0.5

Basic Nutritional Values:

- Calories 180 (Calories from Fat 70)
- Total Fat 8 gm (Saturated Fat 2.5 gm, Trans Fat 0.0 gm, Polyunsaturated Fat 1.3 gm, Monounsaturated Fat 3.2 gm)
- Cholesterol 130 mg
- Sodium 485 mg
- Potassium 385 gm
- Total Carb 12 gm
- Dietary Fiber 1 gm
- Sugars 3 gm
- Protein 15 gm
- Phosphorus 175 gm

Eggs à la Shrimp

Yield: 6 servings
Preparation Time: 15 minutes
Cooking Time: 15 minutes
Ingredients:

- ¼ cup finely chopped celery with leaves
- ¼ tsp. pepper
- ¼ tsp. salt
- 1 cup egg substitute
- 1 Tbsp. canola oil
- 3 green onions with tops, sliced, or 1 small onion, chopped fine
- 3 Tbsp. plus ¼ cup white wine, divided
- 4 big eggs
- 4 oz. frozen peas, or fresh
- 4 oz. shrimp, frozen or canned
- fresh parsley

Directions:

1. Preheat electric frying pan to approximately 375°F, or cast-iron frying pan to moderate high.
2. Heat oil in frying pan. Sauté onions, until soft.
3. Put in celery and fry until softened.
4. Put in shrimp and 3 Tbsp. white wine. Cover and steam over low heat for approximately 3 minutes.
5. In a moderate-sized mixing vessel, toss eggs and egg substitute with ¼ cup white wine. Pour into frying pan.
6. Combine the peas and seasonings into the mixture.
7. Turn frying pan to 300°F, or moderate-low. Stir lightly as mixture cooks. Cook just until mixture sets according to your preference.
8. Serve on warm platter surrounded with fresh parsley.

Goes Well With:

- Freshly baked muffins
- Fresh fruit in season

Exchange List Value:

- Lean Meat 2.0
- Fat 1.0

Basic Nutritional Values:

- Calories 135 (Calories from Fat 55)
- Total Fat 6 gm (Saturated Fat 1.3 gm, Trans Fat 0.0 gm, Polyunsaturated Fat 1.4 gm, Monounsaturated Fat 2.8 gm)
- Cholesterol 165 mg
- Sodium 415 mg
- Potassium 195 gm
- Total Carb 4.5 gm
- Dietary Fiber 1 gm
- Sugars 2 gm
- Protein 14 gm
- Phosphorus 145 gm

Fast, Friendly French Toast

Yield: 8 servings
Preparation Time: 15 minutes
Soaking Time: 1–24 hours
Baking Time: 15 minutes
Ingredients:

- ¼ cup sugar
- ½ cup orange juice
- 1 lb. loaf French bread, cut into 1-inch-thick slices
- 1 Tbsp. vanilla extract
- 1½ cups fat-free milk
- 4 eggs
- cinnamon, optional

Directions:

1. Positionbread slices in a 9x13-inch baking pan.
2. In a mixing vessel, whisk milk, eggs, orange juice, sugar, and vanilla together until thoroughly blended.
3. Pour over bread.
4. Cover and place in the refrigerator 1–24 hours, according to your schedule and how much time you have.
5. Heat oven to 400°F. Oil-coat jelly-roll pan.
6. Move bread to pan, making sure slices don't touch. Dust with cinnamon, if you wish.
7. Bake 15 minutes, or until puffy and slightly browned.

Exchange List Value:

- Starch 2.0
- Carbohydrate 1.0
- Lean Meat 1.0

Basic Nutritional Values:

- Calories 250 (Calories from Fat 30)
- Total Fat 4 gm (Saturated Fat 1.1 gm, Trans Fat 0.0 gm, Polyunsaturated Fat 0.9 gm, Monounsaturated Fat 1.1 gm)
- Cholesterol 95 mg
- Sodium 345 mg
- Potassium 210 gm
- Total Carb 43 gm
- Dietary Fiber 1 gm
- Sugars 12 gm
- Protein 11 gm
- Phosphorus 165 gm

Finnish Coffee Cake

Yield: 24 servings, 2-inch square bar per serving
Preparation Time: 10–20 minutes
Baking Time: 30–35 minutes
Ingredients:

- ½ tsp. baking soda
- ½ tsp. salt
- ¾ tsp. baking powder
- 1 cup canola oil
- 1 cup fat-free buttermilk
- 1 tsp. vanilla extract
- 10 Tbsp. Splenda Sugar Blend
- 1–2 Tbsp. hot water, or a bit more
- 1–2 tsp. vanilla extract, according to your taste preference
- 1–3 tsp. cinnamon, according to your taste preference
- 2 cups confectioners' sugar
- 2 cups flour
- 2 eggs, beaten
- 2 Tbsp. Splenda Brown Sugar Blend
- Glaze, optional

Directions:

1. In good-sized mixing vessel, whisk together Splenda, oil, eggs, buttermilk, and 1 tsp. vanilla.
2. In a separate vessel, sift together flour, baking powder, salt, and baking soda.
3. Combine dry ingredients into buttermilk mixture.
4. Pour half of batter into oil-coated 9x13-inch baking dish.
5. Combine together brown sugar and cinnamon in vessel. Drizzle half of mixture over batter.
6. Repeat layers.

7. Bake at 350°F for 30–35 minutes, or until toothpick injected in center comes out unsoiled.
8. If you're using glaze, poke holes in cake with fork while cake is still warm. In a moderate-sized vessel, combine confectioners' sugar, vanilla, and just enough water to make a thin glaze. Drizzle glaze over cake while still warm.

Exchange List Value:

- Starch 0.5
- Carbohydrate 0.5
- Fat 2.0

Basic Nutritional Values:

- Calories 155 (Calories from Fat 90)
- Total Fat 10 gm (Saturated Fat 0.8 gm, Trans Fat 0.0 gm, Polyunsaturated Fat 2.7 gm, Monounsaturated Fat 5.9 gm)
- Cholesterol 15 mg
- Sodium 105 mg
- Potassium 35 gm
- Total Carb 15 gm
- Dietary Fiber 0 gm
- Sugars 6 gm
- Protein 2 gm
- Phosphorus 45 gm

Glazed Cinnamon Biscuits

Yield: 12 servings, 1 biscuit per serving
Preparation Time: approximately half an hour
Baking Time: 18–20 minutes
Ingredients:
Biscuits:

- 2 cups flour
- 4 tsp. baking powder
- ½ tsp. salt
- 2 Tbsp. Splenda Sugar Blend
- 1 tsp. cinnamon
- 6 Tbsp. trans-fat-free tub margarine, divided
- ¾ cup fat-free milk

Glaze:

- 1 cup granulated Splenda
- 2⅔ Tbsp. cornstarch
- ¼ tsp. vanilla extract
- 1⅓ Tbsp. water

Directions:

1. In a big vessel, mix flour, baking powder, salt, sweetener, and cinnamon.
2. Using a pastry cutter or two knives, cut in 4 Tbsp. margarine until mixture looks like coarse crumbs.
3. Mix in milk just until moistened.
4. Turn onto a slightly floured surface. Rub a bit of vegetable oil on your hands to keep dough from sticking to your fingers while kneading.
5. Knead lightly 8–10 times.
6. Roll dough into an 8×11-inch rectangle, ½-inch thick.

7. Melt residual 2 Tbs. margarine and brush 1 Tbsp. over dough.
8. Roll up jelly-roll style, beginning with long end.
9. Chop roll into 12 equal slices.
10. Place slices cut-side down in oil-coated 7×11-inch baking pan. Make 3 rows with 4 slices in each row.
11. Brush slices with residual margarine.
12. Bake at 375°F for approximately 18–20 minutes, or until golden brown.
13. As biscuits bake, prepare the glaze. Blend Splenda and cornstarch in blender to a very fine powder.
14. In a small vessel, stir vanilla and water together and put in the Splenda mixture.
15. As biscuits finish baking, let them cool 5 minutes.
16. Spread with glaze. Serve instantly.

Exchange List Value:

- Starch 1.0
- Carbohydrate 0.5
- Fat 0.5

Basic Nutritional Values:

- Calories 140 (Calories from Fat 40)
- Total Fat 4.5 gm (Saturated Fat 0.9 gm, Trans Fat 0.0 gm, Polyunsaturated Fat 1.8 gm, Monounsaturated Fat 1.4 gm)
- Cholesterol 0 mg
- Sodium 270 mg
- Potassium 50 gm
- Total Carb 23 gm
- Dietary Fiber 1 gm
- Sugars 5 gm
- Protein 3 gm

- Phosphorus 190 gm

Grits—New Mexico Style

Yield: 24 servings
Preparation Time: 20 minutes
Baking Time: 60 minutes 20 minutes
Ingredients:

- ¼ cup trans-fat-free tub margarine, at room temperature
- ¼ tsp. garlic powder
- 1 lb. 75%-less-fat shredded cheddar cheese
- 1½ cups uncooked grits
- 2 tsp. salt
- 3 eggs, separated
- 4-oz. can chopped green chilies, drained
- dash Tabasco sauce

Directions:

1. Cook grits in big pan according to package directions until thick.
2. Chop margarine into chunks and stir in, followed by chilies, cheese, beaten egg yolks, salt, Tabasco sauce, and garlic powder. Keep on stirring until margarine is totally melted.
3. Whisk egg whites until soft peaks are achieved. Fold into hot ingredients.
4. Pour into thoroughly -oil-coated 4-qt. baking dish.
5. Bake at 350°F for 60 minutes and 20 minutes.

Exchange List Value:

- Starch 0.5
- Lean Meat 1.0
- Fat 0.5

Basic Nutritional Values:

- Calories 100 (Calories from Fat 35)
- Total Fat 4 gm (Saturated Fat 1.5 gm, Trans Fat 0.0 gm, Polyunsaturated Fat 0.8 gm, Monounsaturated Fat 1.0 gm)
- Cholesterol 30 mg
- Sodium 360 mg
- Potassium 50 gm
- Total Carb 9 gm
- Dietary Fiber 0 gm
- Sugars 0 gm
- Protein 8 gm
- Phosphorus 110 gm

Healthy Blueberry Muffins

Yield: 18 servings, 1 muffin per serving
Preparation Time: 20 minutes
Baking Time: 20 minutes
Ingredients:

- ¼ cup oat bran
- ¼ cup quick, or old-fashioned, oats
- ¼ cup wheat germ
- ¼ tsp. allspice
- ¼ tsp. nutmeg
- ¼ tsp. salt
- ½ cup chopped walnuts
- ½ cup whole wheat flour
- ½ tsp. cinnamon
- 1 banana, mashed
- 1 cup blueberries, fresh or frozen and partially thawed
- 1 cup buttermilk
- 1 cup flour
- 1 egg
- 1 Tbsp. vegetable oil
- 1 tsp. baking powder
- 1 tsp. baking soda
- 1 tsp. vanilla extract
- 6 Tbsp. Splenda Sugar Blend

Directions:

1. In big vessel, stir together all dry ingredients (through salt) until thoroughly blended.
2. Softly stir in blueberries and walnuts. (Adding the blueberries to dry ingredients first helps to prevent turning the batter blue from any juice.)

3. In a different container, combine mashed banana, buttermilk, egg, oil, and vanilla.
4. Make a hole in dry ingredients. Pour wet ingredients into hole. Combine just until combined.
5. Fill oil-coated muffin cups almost to the top.
6. Bake at 350°F for about 20 minutes, or until toothpick injected in centers of muffins comes out unsoiled
7. You can make this recipe even healthier by using a banana instead of more oil.

Exchange List Value:

- Carbohydrate 1.0
- Fat 1.0

Basic Nutritional Values:

- Calories 115 (Calories from Fat 30)
- Total Fat 4 gm (Saturated Fat 0.4 gm, Trans Fat 0.0 gm, Polyunsaturated Fat 2.1 gm, Monounsaturated Fat 1.0 gm)
- Cholesterol 10 mg
- Sodium 140 mg
- Potassium 120 gm
- Total Carb 18 gm
- Dietary Fiber 2 gm
- Sugars 7 gm
- Protein 3 gm
- Phosphorus 110 gm

Mexican-Style Grits

Yield: 12 servings
Preparation Time: 25 minutes
Cooking Time: 2–6 hours
Preferred Crock-Pot Size: 4-qt.
Ingredients:

- ½ tsp. garlic powder
- 1½ cups instant grits
- 2 4-oz. cans diced chilies
- 2 Tbsp. light, soft tub margarine
- 4 oz. fat-free cheddar cheese, cubed

Directions:

1. Ready the grits in accordance with the package directions.
2. Mix in cheese, garlic powder, and chilies, until cheese is melted.
3. Stir in margarine. Pour into greased Crock Pot.
4. Cover. Cook on High for appriximately 2–3 hours or on Low 4–6 hours.

Exchange List Value:

- Starch 1.0

Basic Nutritional Values:

- Calories 91 (Calories from Fat 9)
- Total Fat 1 gm (Saturated Fat 0.1 gm, Polyunsaturated Fat 0.3 gm, Monounsaturated Fat 0.5 gm)
- Cholesterol 1 mg
- Sodium 167 mg
- Total Carb 16 gm

- Dietary Fiber 2 gm
- Sugars 0 gm
- Protein 5 gm

Morning Maple Muffins

Yield: 18 muffins, 1 muffin per serving
Preparation Time: 15 minutes
Baking Time: 15–20 minutes
Ingredients:
Muffins:

- ¼ cup fat-free sour cream
- ¼ cup maple syrup
- ¼ cup Splenda Brown Sugar Blend
- ½ cup trans-fat-free tub margarine, melted
- ½ tsp. salt
- ½ tsp. vanilla extract
- ¾ cup fat-free milk
- 1 egg
- 2 cups flour
- 2 tsp. baking powder

Topping:

- ½ tsp. cinnamon
- 2 Tbsp. chopped pecans
- 2 Tbsp. trans-fat-free tub margarine
- 3 Tbsp. flour
- 3 Tbsp. sugar

Directions:

1. To make muffins, mix flour, brown sugar blend, baking powder, and salt in a big vessel.
2. In another vessel, mix milk, melted margarine, maple syrup, sour cream, egg, and vanilla.
3. Mix wet ingredients into dry ingredients just until moistened.

4. Fill oil-coated or paper-lined muffin cups ⅔ full.
5. For topping, mix flour, sugar, nuts, and cinnamon.
6. Chop in margarine, using a pastry cutter or two knives, until crumbly.
7. Drizzle over batter in muffin cups.
8. Bake at 400°F for 15–20 minutes, or until a toothpick injected near the center comes out unsoiled.
9. Cool 5 minutes before taking out of pans to wire racks. Serve warm.

Exchange List Value:

- Starch 1.0
- Carbohydrate 0.5
- Fat 1.0

Basic Nutritional Values:

- Calories 140 (Calories from Fat 55)
- Total Fat 6 gm (Saturated Fat 1.2 gm, Trans Fat 0.0 gm, Polyunsaturated Fat 2.2 gm, Monounsaturated Fat 2.0 gm)
- Cholesterol 10 mg
- Sodium 165 mg
- Potassium 60 gm
- Total Carb 20 gm
- Dietary Fiber 1 gm
- Sugars 6 gm
- Protein 3 gm
- Phosphorus 90 gm

Oatmeal Morning

Yield: 6 servings
Preparation Time: 10 minutes
Cooking Time: 2½–6 hours
Preferred Crock-Pot Size: 3-qt.
Ingredients:

- 1 cup uncooked steel-cut oats
- 1 cup dried cranberries
- 1 cup walnuts
- ½ tsp. salt
- 1 Tbsp. cinnamon
- 2 cups fat-free milk
- 2 cups water

Directions:

1. Mix all dry ingredients in Crock Pot. Stir thoroughly.
2. Pour in milk and water. Combine together thoroughly
3. Cover. Cook on High for approximately 150 minutes, or on Low 5–6 hours.

Exchange List Value:

- Bread/Starch 3.0
- Fruit 2.0
- Fat 1.0

Basic Nutritional Values:

- Calories 275 (Calories from Fat 125)
- Total Fat 14 gm (Saturated Fat 1.5 gm, Polyunsaturated Fat 10.0 gm, Monounsaturated Fat 2.0 gm)
- Cholesterol 0 mg

- Sodium 235 mg
- Total Carb 34 gm
- Dietary Fiber 4 gm
- Sugars 18 gm
- Protein 8 gm

Oatmeal Pancakes

Yield: 6 servings, 1 pancake per serving
Preparation Time: 5 minutes
Cooking Time: 10 minutes
Ingredients:

- ¼ cup fat-free milk
- ½ cup dry oats, rolled or quick-cooking
- ½ cup flour
- ½ tsp. baking soda
- ¾ cup fat-free buttermilk
- 1 egg, beaten
- 1 Tbsp. Splenda
- 1 tsp. baking powder
- 2 Tbsp. canola oil

Directions:

1. Mix flour, oats, Splenda, baking powder, and baking soda in a big mixing vessel.
2. In a separate vessel, mix buttermilk, milk, oil, and egg until smooth.
3. Combine wet ingredients into dry ingredients, until barely moistened.
4. Drop by a small amount of half-cupfuls into frying pan or onto griddle.
5. Cook until small bubbles appear on top.
6. Turn over and cook until slighly browned.

Exchange List Value:

- Starch 1.0
- Fat 1.0

Basic Nutritional Values:

- Calories 140 (Calories from Fat 55)
- Total Fat 6 gm (Saturated Fat 0.7 gm, Trans Fat 0.0 gm, Polyunsaturated Fat 1.7 gm, Monounsaturated Fat 3.4 gm)
- Cholesterol 30 mg
- Sodium 215 mg
- Potassium 110 gm
- Total Carb 17 gm
- Dietary Fiber 1 gm
- Sugars 4 gm
- Protein 4 gm
- Phosphorus 170 gm

Overnight Apple French Toast

Yield: 9 servings, 1 slice per serving
Preparation Time: 40–45 minutes
Chilling Time: 8 hours, or overnight
Baking Time: 35–40 minutes
Ingredients:

- 1 cup fat-free milk
- 1 tsp. vanilla extract
- 3 eggs
- 3 Tbsp. trans-fat-free tub margarine
- 3–4 big tart apples, peeled and sliced ¼-inch thick
- 6 Tbsp. Splenda Brown Sugar Blend
- 9 slices day-old French bread, ¾-inch thick, about 1 oz. each

Syrup:

- ¼ cup apple jelly
- ¼ tsp. cinnamon
- ½ cup unsweetened applesauce
- 1/8 tsp. ground cloves
- maple syrup for serving, optional
- sprinkle nutmeg, optional
- whipped cream, optional

Directions:

1. In a small saucepan, melt Splenda and margarine together about 3–4 minutes, stirring continuously, until lightly thick.
2. Pour into non-oil-coated 9x13-inch baking pan.
3. Top with apple slices.
4. In a moderate-sized mixing vessel, whisk together eggs, milk, and vanilla.

5. Dip bread slices in egg mixture, one after another, and then place over top of apples.
6. Cover and place in the refrigerator overnight.
7. Take out from refrigerator approximately half an hour before baking. Drizzle with nutmeg if you wish.
8. Bake with an open lid at 350°F for 35–40 minutes.
9. In the meantime, prepare syrup by cooking applesauce, cinnamon, apple jelly, and ground cloves in small saucepan until hot.
10. Serve over toast.
11. Offer maple syrup and whipped cream as toppings, if you wish.

Exchange List Value:

- Starch 1.0
- Fruit 1.0
- Carbohydrate 1.0
- Fat 1.0

Basic Nutritional Values:

- Calories 245 (Calories from Fat 45)
- Total Fat 5 gm (Saturated Fat 1.3 gm, Trans Fat 0.0 gm, Polyunsaturated Fat 1.8 gm, Monounsaturated Fat 1.6 gm)
- Cholesterol 65 mg
- Sodium 220 mg
- Potassium 195 gm
- Total Carb 43 gm
- Dietary Fiber 2 gm
- Sugars 19 gm
- Protein 7 gm
- Phosphorus 105 gm

Peanut Butter Granola

Yield: 26 servings
Preparation Time: 20 minutes
Cooking Time: 1½ hours
Preferred Crock-Pot Size: 5-qt.
Ingredients:

- ¼ cup toasted coconut
- ½ cup brown sugar substitute to equal 4 Tbsp. sugar
- ½ cup raisins
- ½ cup sunflower seeds
- ½ cup wheat germ
- ¾ cup peanut butter
- 6 cups dry oatmeal
- 8 Tbsp. light, soft tub margarine

Directions:

1. Mix oatmeal, wheat germ, coconut, sunflower seeds, and raisins in big Crock Pot.
2. Melt together margarine, peanut butter, and brown sugar. Pour over oatmeal in cooker. Combine thoroughly.
3. Cover. Cook on Low for approximately 90 minutes, stirring every 15 minutes.
4. Let cool in cooker, stirring every 30 minutes or so, or spread onto cookie sheet. When completely cooled, break into chunks and store in airtight container.

Exchange List Value:

- Starch 0.5
- Carbohydrate 1.0
- Fat 1.5

Basic Nutritional Values:

- Calories 179 (Calories from Fat 73)
- Total Fat 8 gm (Saturated Fat 1.5 gm, Polyunsaturated Fat 2.8 gm, Monounsaturated Fat 3.3 gm)
- Cholesterol 0 mg
- Sodium 70 mg
- Total Carb 22 gm
- Dietary Fiber 3 gm
- Sugars 7 gm
- Protein 6 gm

Potato-Bacon Gratin

Yield: 8 servings, about 5 oz. per serving
Preparation Time: 15 minutes
Baking Time: 60 minutes
Standing Time: 10 minutes
Ingredients:

- 1 clove garlic, minced
- 1 cup lower-sodium, lower-fat chicken broth
- 1 Tbsp. olive oil
- 4 big potatoes, peeled or unpeeled, divided
- 5-oz. reduced-fat grated Swiss cheddar, divided
- 6-oz. bag fresh spinach
- 6-oz. Canadian bacon slices, divided

Directions:

1. In big frying pan, fry spinach and garlic in olive oil just until spinach is wilted.
2. Chop potatoes into thin slices.
3. In 2-qt. baking dish, layer ⅓ the potatoes, half the bacon, ⅓ the cheese, and half the wilted spinach.
4. Repeat layers ending with potatoes. Save ⅓ cheese for later.
5. Pour chicken broth over all.
6. Cover and bake at 350°F for approximately 45 minutes.
7. Uncover and bake 15 more minutes. During final 5 minutes, top with cheese.
8. Letstand 10 minutes before serving.

Goes Well With:

- Baked apples or applesauce

Exchange List Value:

- Carbohydrate 2.0
- Lean Meat 2.0

Basic Nutritional Values:

- Calories 220 (Calories from Fat 65)
- Total Fat 7 gm (Saturated Fat 2.4 gm, Trans Fat 0.0 gm, Polyunsaturated Fat 0.5 gm, Monounsaturated Fat 2.7 gm)
- Cholesterol 25 mg
- Sodium 415 mg
- Potassium 710 gm
- Total Carb 28 gm
- Dietary Fiber 3 gm
- Sugars 2 gm
- Protein 14 gm
- Phosphorus 285 gm

Quiche

Yield: 6 servings, 1 slice of the pie per serving
Preparation Time: 25 minutes
Cooking/Baking *Time:* 55–65 minutes
Standing Time: 5–10 minutes
Ingredients:

- ½ cup chopped chicken breast
- ½ cup egg substitute
- ½ cup grated reduced-fat Swiss cheese
- ½ tsp. basil, sage, thyme, or oregano
- ¾ tsp. salt
- 1 cup fat-free evaporated milk
- 2 cups chopped tomatoes, green beans, onions, or mushrooms
- 2 Tbsp. flour
- 9-inch unbaked pie shell
- dash pepper

Directions:

1. Bake pie shell for approximately 10 minutes at 375°F. Set aside.
2. Lightly fry choice of vegetables and chicken. Ladle into pie shell.
3. Drizzle choice of seasonings over vegetable mixture. Put in salt and dash of pepper. Cover with grated cheese.
4. Mix egg substitute, flour, and milk. Pour over ingredients.
5. Bake at 375°F for approximately 40–45 minutes or until set. Allow to sit at least 5 minutes before serving.

Exchange List Value:

- Carbohydrate 1.0

- Lean Meat 2.0

Basic Nutritional Values:

- Calories 160 (Calories from Fat 45)
- Total Fat 5 gm (Saturated Fat 1.5 gm, Trans Fat 0.2 gm, Polyunsaturated Fat 0.8 gm, Monounsaturated Fat 1.8 gm)
- Cholesterol 20 mg
- Sodium 430 mg
- Potassium 365 gm
- Total Carb 16 gm
- Dietary Fiber 1 gm
- Sugars 7 gm
- Protein 13 gm
- Phosphorus 195 gm

Sausage and Eggs Baked in Mugs

Yield: 10 servings

Preparation Time: approximately half an hour

Baking Time: 25–30 minutes for mugs or ramekins; 60 minutes for 9x13-inch baking dish

Ingredients:

- ½ cup fat-free buttermilk
- ¾ cup shredded 75%-less-fat sharp cheddar cheese
- 1 Tbsp. Dijon mustard
- 10¾-oz. can cream of mushroom soup
- 12 oz. sourdough bread, sliced and cut into ½-inch cubes
- 2½ cups fat-free milk
- 4 big eggs
- 6 oz. 50%-reduced-fat pork bulk sausage

Directions:

1. Coat insides of 10 ovenproof coffee mugs or ramekins with nonstick cooking spray.
2. Separate bread cubes uniformly among mugs or ramekins.
3. Brown bulk sausage in frying pan, breaking up with wooden spoon and stirring until all pink is gone. Eliminate drippings.
4. Crown bread cubes in each mug or ramekin with crumbled sausage.
5. In a mixing vessel, whisk together milk, eggs, and Dijon mustard. Pour uniformly over bread and sausage.
6. In same vessel, whisk together buttermilk and cream of mushroom soup. Spoon over bread mixture.
7. Drizzle each mug or ramekin with cheddar cheese.
8. Put coffee mugs or ramekins on baking sheet.
9. Bake at 350°F for approximately 25–30 minutes, or until each casserole is set and puffed. Serve instantly.

Exchange List Value:

- Starch 1.0
- Carbohydrate 0.5
- Lean Meat 2.0
- Fat 0.5

Basic Nutritional Values:

- Calories 225 (Calories from Fat 55)
- Total Fat 6 gm (Saturated Fat 2.3 gm, Trans Fat 0.0 gm, Polyunsaturated Fat 1.3 gm, Monounsaturated Fat 2.4 gm)
- Cholesterol 90 mg
- Sodium 525 mg
- Potassium 435 gm
- Total Carb 26 gm
- Dietary Fiber 1 gm
- Sugars 5 gm
- Protein 15 gm
- Phosphorus 225 gm

Shredded Potato Omelet

Yield: 6 servings
Preparation Time: 15 minutes
Cooking Time: 20 minutes
Ingredients:

- ⅛ tsp. black pepper
- ¼ cup fat-free milk
- ¼ cup minced green bell pepper
- ¼ cup minced onion
- ¼ tsp. salt
- 1 cup 75%-less-fat shredded cheddar cheese
- 1 cup egg substitute
- 2 cups shredded cooked potatoes
- 3 slices bacon
- cooking spray

Directions:

1. In big frying pan, fry bacon until crunchy. Take out bacon and crumble. Wipe frying pan, and spray slightly with cooking spray.
2. Combine potatoes, onion, and green pepper in vessel. Spoon into frying pan. Cook over low heat—without stirring—until underside is crunchy and brown.
3. Blend egg substitute, milk, salt, and pepper in mixing vessel. Pour over potato mixture.
4. Top with cheese and bacon.
5. Cover. Cook over low heat about 10 minutes, or until set. Loosen omelet and serve.

Exchange List Value:

- Starch 1.0

- Lean Meat 1.0

Basic Nutritional Values:

- Calories 130 (Calories from Fat 25)
- Total Fat 3 gm (Saturated Fat 1.4 gm, Trans Fat 0.0 gm, Polyunsaturated Fat 0.2 gm, Monounsaturated Fat 0.9 gm)
- Cholesterol 10 mg
- Sodium 415 mg
- Potassium 280 gm
- Total Carb 13 gm
- Dietary Fiber 2 gm
- Sugars 2 gm
- Protein 12 gm
- Phosphorus 150 gm

Southwest Brunch Casserole

Yield: 4 servings, ½ an English muffin per serving
Preparation Time: 20–30 minutes
Chilling Time: 3–8 hours
Baking Time: 20–25 minutes
Ingredients:

- ¼ cup chopped chilies, optional
- ¼ cup fat-free sour cream
- ¼ cup grated 75%-less-fat cheddar cheese
- 1 cup egg substitute
- 1 oz. reduced-fat bulk pork sausage
- 1 Tbsp. trans-fat-free tub margarine
- 2 English muffins, split

Directions:

1. Disperse the margarine over cut sides of each muffin half. Place margarine-side up in 8-inch square baking pan covered with nonstick cooking spray.
2. In a small frying pan, cook sausage. Drain off drippings.
3. Spoon sausage over muffin halves.
4. In a small mixing vessel, whisk egg substitute and sour cream together.
5. Pour over sausage.
6. Drizzle with cheese, and chilies if you wish.
7. Cover and place in the refrigerator 3 hours or overnight.
8. Take out from refrigerator approximately half an hour before baking.
9. Bake with an open lid at 350°F for approximately 20–25 minutes, or until knife injected near center comes out unsoiled.

Exchange List Value:

- Starch 1.0
- Lean Meat 1.0
- Fat 0.5

Basic Nutritional Values:

- Calories 160 (Calories from Fat 40)
- Total Fat 4.5 gm (Saturated Fat 1.5 gm, Trans Fat 0.0 gm, Polyunsaturated Fat 1.2 gm, Monounsaturated Fat 1.5 gm)
- Cholesterol 10 mg
- Sodium 365 mg
- Potassium 170 gm
- Total Carb 16 gm
- Dietary Fiber 1 gm
- Sugars 2 gm
- Protein 13 gm
- Phosphorus 95 gm

Southwestern Egg Casserole
Yield: 12 servings, about 3x3-inch square per serving
Preparation Time: 20–30 minutes
Baking Time: 35–45 minutes
Standing Time: 5–10 minutes
Ingredients:

- ⅛ tsp. pepper
- ⅛ tsp. salt
- ¼ cup trans-fat-free tub margarine
- ½ cup flour
- 1 tsp. baking powder
- 1½ cups shredded 75%-less-fat sharp cheddar cheese
- 2 4-oz. cans chopped green chilies
- 2 cups fat-free cottage cheese
- 2½ cups egg substitute

Directions:

1. Beat egg substitute in a big mixing vessel.
2. In a smaller vessel, mix flour, baking powder, salt, and pepper. Stir into egg substitute. Batter will be lumpy.
3. Put the cheeses, margarine, and chilies into batter.
4. Pour into oil-coated 9x13-inch baking dish.
5. Bake at 350°F for 35–45 minutes, or until knife injected near center comes out unsoiled.
6. Allow to stand 5–10 minutes before cutting.

Exchange List Value:

- Carbohydrate 0.5
- Lean Meat 2.0

Basic Nutritional Values:

- Calories 130 (Calories from Fat 35)
- Total Fat 4 gm (Saturated Fat 1.4 gm, Trans Fat 0.0 gm, Polyunsaturated Fat 1.2 gm, Monounsaturated Fat 1.2 gm)
- Cholesterol 10 mg
- Sodium 450 mg
- Potassium 180 gm
- Total Carb 9 gm
- Dietary Fiber 1 gm
- Sugars 1 gm
- Protein 14 gm
- Phosphorus 190 gm

Sticky Buns

Yield: 15 buns, 1 bun per serving
Preparation Time: 35 minutes
Rising Time: approximately half an hour
Baking Time: 15 minutes
Ingredients:

Dough:

- ¼ cup sugar
- ½ cup warm water
- ¾ cup milk
- 1 egg, beaten
- 1 Tbsp. yeast
- 1 tsp. salt
- 2 Tbsp. canola oil
- 2 Tbsp. trans-fat-free tub margarine
- 3 cups flour

Sauce:

- ⅓ cup pecans
- ½ cup Splenda Brown Sugar Blend
- ¾ tsp. cinnamon
- 1 Tbsp. water
- 6 Tbsp. trans-fat-free tub margarine

Directions:

1. In a small vessel, stir yeast into warm water until blended. Set aside.
2. Heat milk, margarine, and oil in moderate-sized saucepan over low heat until margarine becomes molten. Turn off the heat.
3. Stir salt and sugar into milk mixture until blended.

4. Mix yeast water, egg, and flour into other ingredients.
5. Place in warm place and allow to rise for approximately half an hour.
6. In the meantime, ready sauce. In a moderate-sized saucepan, heat margarine, cinnamon, Splenda, and water together. Make good and hot, but do not let boil.
7. Mix in pecans.
8. Pour sauce into thoroughly -oil-coated 9×13-inch baking pan. Spread over bottom of pan.
9. Stir down batter. Ladle by tablespoons over sauce. Make about 12-15 buns.
10. Bake at 350°F for approximately 15 minutes.
11. Allow to cool for 1 minute.
12. Coat baking pan with rimmed cookie sheet. Flip over cautiously to release sticky buns onto cookie sheet.

Exchange List Value:

- Starch 1.5
- Carbohydrate 0.5
- Fat 1.5

Basic Nutritional Values:

- Calories 210 (Calories from Fat 70)
- Total Fat 8 gm (Saturated Fat 1.3 gm, Trans Fat 0.0 gm, Polyunsaturated Fat 2.9 gm, Monounsaturated Fat 3.8 gm)
- Cholesterol 15 mg
- Sodium 210 mg
- Potassium 85 gm
- Total Carb 30 gm
- Dietary Fiber 1 gm
- Sugars 7 gm
- Protein 4 gm

- Phosphorus 65 gm

Strawberry Muffins

Yield: 14 muffins, 1 muffin per serving
Preparation Time: 10–15 minutes
Standing Time: approximately half an hour
Baking Time: 10–12 minutes
Ingredients:

- ¼ cup trans-fat-free tub margarine
- ¼ tsp. nutmeg
- ¼ tsp. salt
- ½ tsp. baking soda
- 1 tsp. vanilla extract
- 1½ cups mashed strawberries
- 1¾ cups flour
- 2 eggs, beaten
- 6 Tbsp. Splenda Sugar Blend, divided

Directions:

1. In a small mixing vessel, mix strawberries and 2 Tbsp. sweetener. Set aside for approximately half an hour. Drain strawberries, reserving liquid.
2. In a big mixing vessel, mix flour, nutmeg, salt, and baking soda. Set aside.
3. In yet another vessel, combine eggs, melted margarine, vanilla, 4 Tbsp. sweetener, and juice from berries.
4. Put into flour mixture, stirring just until blended.
5. Fold in berries.
6. Spoon batter into oil-coated muffin tins.
7. Bake at 425°F for 10–12 minutes, or until toothpick injected in centers of muffins comes out unsoiled.

Exchange List Value:

- Carbohydrate 1.5
- Fat 0.5

Basic Nutritional Values:

- Calories 120 (Calories from Fat 30)
- Total Fat 4 gm (Saturated Fat 0.8 gm, Trans Fat 0.0 gm, Polyunsaturated Fat 1.2 gm, Monounsaturated Fat 1.1 gm)
- Cholesterol 25 mg
- Sodium 120 mg
- Potassium 65 gm
- Total Carb 19 gm
- Dietary Fiber 1 gm
- Sugars 7 gm
- Protein 3 gm
- Phosphorus 40 gm

Waffles with Cinnamon Apple Syrup

Yield: 12 5-inch waffles and 1¾ cups syrup, 1 waffle and 2⅓ Tbsp. syrup per serving

Preparation Time: 15 minutes

Cooking Time: Approximately 3 minutes per waffle

Ingredients:

Waffles:

- 2 cups flour
- 2 Tbsp. sugar
- 3 tsp. baking powder
- ½ tsp. salt
- 2 eggs
- 1½ cups fat-free milk
- 4 Tbsp. canola oil

Cinnamon Apple Syrup:

- 2 Tbsp. cornstarch
- ½ tsp. cinnamon
- ⅛ tsp. salt
- 1 cup water
- ¾ cup unsweetened apple juice concentrate
- ½ tsp. vanilla extract

Directions:

1. To make waffles, mix flour, sugar, baking powder, and salt together in big vessel.
2. In a separate vessel, whisk eggs, milk, and oil together.
3. Put the wet ingredients into dry ingredients. Beat just until blended.
4. Pour a slight amount of ½ cup batter onto hot waffle iron. Cook in accordance with your waffle iron's instructions.

5. To make syrup, mix cornstarch, cinnamon, and salt in saucepan.
6. Progressively stir in water and apple juice concentrate until smooth.
7. Over moderate heat, and stirring constantly, bring to boil.
8. Cook, stirring constantly, for 2 minutes, or until thickened.
9. Turn off the heat. Combine in vanilla.
10. Serve warm over waffles.

Exchange List Value:

- Starch 1.0
- Carbohydrate 1.0
- Fat 1.0

Basic Nutritional Values:

- Calories 180 (Calories from Fat 55)
- Total Fat 6 gm (Saturated Fat 0.6 gm, Trans Fat 0.0 gm, Polyunsaturated Fat 1.6 gm, Monounsaturated Fat 3.3 gm)
- Cholesterol 30 mg
- Sodium 240 mg
- Potassium 145 gm
- Total Carb 28 gm
- Dietary Fiber 1 gm
- Sugars 11 gm
- Protein 4 gm
- Phosphorus 185 gm

Zucchini Oatmeal Muffins

Yield: 30 muffins, 1 muffin per serving
Preparation Time: 15 minutes
Baking Time: 20–25 minutes
Ingredients:

- ½ cup dry oatmeal, quick or old-fashioned
- ¾ cup canola oil
- ¾ cup Splenda Sugar Blend
- 1 cup chopped walnuts
- 1 Tbsp. baking powder
- 1 tsp. cinnamon
- 1 tsp. salt
- 10 oz. zucchini (1¼ cups shredded), peeled or unpeeled
- 2½ cups flour
- 4 eggs

Directions:

1. Combine flour, sweetener, dry oatmeal, baking powder, salt, cinnamon, and walnuts together in a big mixing vessel.
2. In a different vessel, mix eggs, zucchini, and oil.
3. Mix wet ingredients into dry ingredients, until just combined. Do not over-stir.
4. Fill oil-coated baking tins half-full. (Or use paper liners instead of greasing tins.)
5. Bake at 400°F for 20–25 minutes, or until toothpick injected in centers of muffins comes out unsoiled.

Exchange List Value:

- Carbohydrate 1.0
- Fat 2.0

Basic Nutritional Values:

- Calories 150 (Calories from Fat 80)
- Total Fat 9 gm (Saturated Fat 0.9 gm, Trans Fat 0.0 gm, Polyunsaturated Fat 3.6 gm, Monounsaturated Fat 4.1 gm)
- Cholesterol 25 mg
- Sodium 125 mg
- Potassium 70 gm
- Total Carb 15 gm
- Dietary Fiber 1 gm
- Sugars 5 gm
- Protein 3 gm
- Phosphorus 95 gm

Breads

Bread is a staple food prepared from a dough of flour and water, most commonly by baking. Throughout recorded history it has been a vital food in large parts of the world and is one of the oldest man-made foods, having been of momentous importance since the dawn of agriculture.

It is a misconception that diabetics cannot enjoy this staple food. The bread recipes that follow have neem engineered keeping a diabetic's nutritional restrictions in mind. However, constraint must be practices as excess of everything is bad. Use the nutritional info below every recipe, and make sure you eat within the allowed limitations for you.

Banana Bread

Yield: 15 servings, 1 slice per serving
Preparation Time: 25 minutes
Baking Time: 50 minutes
Cooling Time: approximately half an hour
Ingredients:

- ¼ cup hot water
- ¼ tsp. salt
- ⅓ cup canola oil
- 1 cup chopped walnuts
- 1¼ tsp. baking soda
- 2 cups whole wheat flour
- 2 eggs, beaten
- 6 moderate bananas, mashed

Directions:

1. Beat oil and eggs and mix thoroughly. Stir in bananas.
2. Sift together all dry ingredients and add to batter, alternating with hot water. Combine until smooth. Fold in the walnuts.
3. Bake in oil-coated loaf pan at 325°F for Approximately 50 minutes.
4. Cool on wire rack for ½ hour before slicing.
5. Serving suggestion:
6. Serve with honey or maple syrup

Exchange List Value:

- Carbohydrate 1.5
- Fat 2.0

Basic Nutritional Values:

- Calories 205 (Calories from Fat 100)
- Total Fat 11 gm (Saturated Fat 1.2 gm, Trans Fat 0.0 gm, Polyunsaturated Fat 5.4 gm, Monounsaturated Fat 4.0 gm)
- Cholesterol 25 mg
- Sodium 155 mg
- Potassium 290 gm
- Total Carb 24 gm
- Dietary Fiber 4 gm
- Sugars 6 gm
- Protein 5 gm
- Phosphorus 105 gm

Banana Loaf

Yield: 10 servings
Preparation Time: 20 minutes
Cooking Time: 2–2½ hours
Preferred Slow Cooler Size: 4- or 5-qt.
Ingredients:

- ¼ cup margarine, softened
- ½ cup sugar substitute to equal ¼ cup sugar
- 1 cup flour
- 1 tsp. baking soda
- 1 tsp. vanilla
- 2 eggs
- 3 very ripe, moderate bananas

Directions:

1. Mix all ingredients in an electric mixing vessel. Beat 2 minutes or until thoroughly blended. Pour into thoroughly -oil-coated 2-lb. coffee can or 9×5-inch loaf pan.
2. Place can/pan in Crock Pot. Cover can/pan with 6 layers of paper towels between cooker lid and bread.
3. Cover cooker. Bake on High 2–2½ hours, or until toothpick injected in center comes out unsoiled. Cool 15 minutes before taking out of pan.

Exchange List Value:

- Carbohydrate 2.0
- Fat 1.0

Basic Nutritional Values:

- Calories 177 (Calories from Fat 53)
- Total Fat 6 gm (Saturated Fat 1.3 gm, Polyunsaturated Fat 1.7 gm, Monounsaturated Fat 2.5 gm)
- Cholesterol 43 mg
- Sodium 192 mg
- Total Carb 29 gm
- Dietary Fiber 1 gm
- Sugars 16 gm
- Protein 3 gm

Boston Brown Bread

Yield: 3 loaves, 7 servings per loaf
Preparation Time: 45 minutes
Cooking Time: 4 hours
Preferred Slow Cooker Size: 6-qt.
Ingredients:

- ⅓ cup molasses
- ½ cup chopped walnuts
- ½ cup raisins
- ½ cup rye flour
- ½ cup whole wheat flour
- ½ cup yellow cornmeal
- ¾ tsp. salt
- 1 cup low-fat buttermilk
- 1 tsp. baking soda
- 3 16-oz. vegetable cans, emptied and cleaned, lids and labels discarded
- 3 Tbsp. sugar

Directions:

1. Spray insides of vegetable cans with nonstick cooking spray. Spray three 6-inch-square pieces of foil also with the cooking spray. Set aside.
2. Mix rye flour, cornmeal, whole wheat flour, sugar, baking soda, and salt in a big vessel.
3. Stir in walnuts and raisins.
4. Whisk together buttermilk and molasses. Add to dry ingredients. Stir until thoroughly combined. Spoon into prepared cans.

5. Place one piece of foil, oil-coated side down, on top of each can. Secure foil with rubber bands or cotton string. Place upright in Crock Pot.
6. Pour boiling water into Crock Pot to come halfway up sides of cans. Make sure foil tops do not touch boiling water.
7. Cover cooker. Cook on Low 4 hours, or until skewer injected in center of bread comes out unsoiled.
8. To remove bread, lay cans on their sides. Roll and tap lightly on all sides until bread releases. Cool totally on wire racks.
9. Serving suggestion:
10. Serve with butter or cream cheese and vessels of soup.

Exchange List Value::

- Carbohydrate 1.0
- Fat 0.5

Basic Nutritional Values:

- Calories 85 (Calories from Fat 20)
- Total Fat 2 gm (Saturated Fat 0.2 gm, Polyunsaturated Fat 1.4 gm, Monounsaturated Fat 0.3 gm)
- Cholesterol 0 mg
- Sodium 158 mg
- Total Carb 16 gm
- Dietary Fiber 2 gm
- Sugars 8 gm
- Protein 2 gm

Cheddar Biscuits

Yield: 12 servings, 1 biscuit per serving
Preparation Time: 10–20 minutes
Baking Time: 15–17 minutes
Ingredients:

- ¼ tsp. dried parsley flakes
- ½ tsp. garlic powder, divided
- ¾ cup fat-free milk
- 1 cup 75%-less-fat shredded cheddar cheese
- 2½ cups reduced-fat baking mix
- 4 Tbsp. trans-fat-free tub margarine
- butter-flavored cooking spray

Directions:

1. In good-sized mixing vessel, cut margarine into baking mix using pastry cutter or 2 forks. Mix until mixture looks like small peas.
2. Stir in cheese, milk, and ¼ tsp. garlic powder until just blended. Do not over-mix.
3. Drop batter by ¼ cupfuls onto oil-coated baking sheet. (An ice cream scoop works thoroughly.)
4. Bake 15–17 minutes at 400°F, or until tops are slightly browned.
5. Take out from oven. Spray tops slightly with cooking spray, 6 short sprays total. Drizzle uniformly with ¼ tsp. garlic powder and parsley flakes. Serve warm.

Exchange List Value:

- Starch 1.0
- Fat 1.0

Basic Nutritional Values:

- Calories 140 (Calories from Fat 45)
- Total Fat 5 gm (Saturated Fat 1.3 gm, Trans Fat 0.0 gm, Polyunsaturated Fat 1.5 gm, Monounsaturated Fat 2.1 gm)
- Cholesterol 5 mg
- Sodium 370 mg
- Potassium 65 gm
- Total Carb 18 gm
- Dietary Fiber 1 gm
- Sugars 3 gm
- Protein 5 gm
- Phosphorus 210 gm

Cheesy Garlic Bread

Yield: 12 servings, 1 slice per serving
Preparation Time: 15 minutes
Baking Time: 10 minutes
Ingredients:

- ½ Tbsp. finely chopped onion
- ½ tsp. garlic powder
- ½ tsp. salt
- 1 Tbsp. Italian seasoning
- 16-oz. loaf French bread
- 4 Tbsp. freshly grated Parmesan cheese
- 4 Tbsp. trans-fat-free tub margarine

Directions:

1. Warm margarine until softened. Stir in all residual ingredients except bread.
2. Slice bread and spread mixture thinly on each slice.
3. Warm in microwave or slow oven (200–300°F) until margarine melts instantly before serving.

Exchange List Value:

- Starch 1.5
- Fat 0.5

Cocoa Zucchini Bread

Yield: 2 loaves, 16 slices per loaf, 1 slice per serving
Preparation Time: 15 minutes
Baking Time: 60 minutes
Cooling Time: 45–50 minutes
Ingredients:

- ¼ cup cocoa powder, optional
- ½ cup chopped walnuts, or pecans
- ½ cup fat-free milk
- ½ cup mini-chocolate chips
- ½ tsp. salt
- 1 cup canola oil
- 1 cup Splenda Sugar Blend
- 1 tsp. baking powder
- 1 tsp. baking soda
- 1 tsp. cinnamon
- 1 tsp. vanilla extract
- 2 cups grated zucchini
- 3 cups flour
- 3 eggs

Directions:

1. Blend Splenda, eggs, and oil in big mixing vessel.
2. Stir in zucchini.
3. Add milk and vanilla and stir thoroughly.
4. Combine flour, cinnamon, baking soda, baking powder, salt, and cocoa powder (if you wish) together in moderate-sized mixing vessel.
5. Add dry ingredients to zucchini mixture. Stir completely.
6. Add in chocolate chips and nuts. Stir.

7. Pour into two oil-coated 9×5-inch loaf pans. Bake at 350°F for 60 minutes. Test that bread is finished by inserting toothpick into center of each loaf. If pick comes out unsoiled, bread is done. If it doesn't, continue baking 3–5 minutes. Test again.
8. Allow to cool in pans 15–20 minutes.
9. Take out from pans. Allow to stand approximately half an hour or more before slicing and serving.

Exchange List Value:

- Carbohydrate 1.0
- Fat 2.0

Basic Nutritional Values:

1. Calories 160 (Calories from Fat 80)
2. Total Fat 9 gm (Saturated Fat 1.3 gm, Trans Fat 0.0 gm, Polyunsaturated Fat 3.0 gm, Monounsaturated Fat 4.9 gm)
3. Cholesterol 20 mg
4. Sodium 95 mg
5. Potassium 60 gm
6. Total Carb 18 gm
7. Dietary Fiber 1 gm
8. Sugars 8 gm
9. Protein 2 gm
10. Phosphorus 55 gm

Corn Sticks

Yield: 20 servings
Preparation Time: 25 minutes
Baking Time: 10–12 minutes
Ingredients:

- ¼ cup freshly grated Parmesan cheese
- 1 Tbsp. dill seed
- 1 tsp. powdered garlic
- 2 cups reduced-fat baking mix
- 4 Tbsp. trans-fat-free tub margarine, melted
- 8½-oz. can cream-style corn

Directions:

1. Mix baking mix, corn, Parmesan cheese, garlic, and dill seed and mix thoroughly.
2. Knead 15–20 strokes on slightly floured on slightly floured board. Roll into big rectangle with rolling pin.
3. Chop into 1×3-inch strips. Place strips 1½ inches apart on non-oil-coated cookie sheet. Brush with melted margarine.
4. Bake at 450°F for 10–12 minutes.

Exchange List Value:

- Starch 0.5
- Fat 0.5

Basic Nutritional Values:

- Calories 70 (Calories from Fat 20)
- Total Fat 2.5 gm (Saturated Fat 0.6 gm, Trans Fat 0.0 gm, Polyunsaturated Fat 0.9 gm, Monounsaturated Fat 1.1 gm)

- Cholesterol 0 mg
- Sodium 185 mg
- Potassium 35 gm
- Total Carb 10 gm
- Dietary Fiber 0 gm
- Sugars 2 gm
- Protein 1 gm
- Phosphorus 85 gm

Cornbread

Yield: 16 servings, 2×2-inch square per serving
Preparation Time: 10 minutes
Baking Time: 35 minutes
Ingredients:

- ½ cup buttermilk
- ½ cup fat-free sour cream
- ½ tsp. baking powder
- ½ tsp. salt
- 1 cup cornmeal
- 1 cup flour
- 1 tsp. baking soda
- 2 eggs, beaten
- 5⅓ Tbsp. trans-fat-free tub margarine, softened
- 6 Tbsp. Splenda Sugar Blend

Directions:

1. Cream Splenda and margarine together thoroughly.
2. Combine in sour cream and buttermilk, and eggs. Combine thoroughly again.
3. In a separate vessel, mix flour, cornmeal, salt, baking soda, and baking powder.
4. Add dry ingredients to creamed mixture. Stir as little as possible.
5. Pour batter into oil-coated 8×8-inch baking dish.
6. Bake at 350°F for 35 minutes, or until toothpick injected in center comes out unsoiled.

Exchange List Value:

- Starch 1.0

- Fat 0.5

Basic Nutritional Values:

- Calories 120 (Calories from Fat 30)
- Total Fat 4 gm (Saturated Fat 0.9 gm, Trans Fat 0.0 gm, Polyunsaturated Fat 1.4 gm, Monounsaturated Fat 1.2 gm)
- Cholesterol 25 mg
- Sodium 210 mg
- Potassium 40 gm
- Total Carb 19 gm
- Dietary Fiber 1 gm
- Sugars 5 gm
- Protein 3 gm
- Phosphorus 50 gm

Cornbread from Scratch

Yield: 9 servings
Preparation Time: 15 minutes
Cooking Time: 2–3 hours
Preferred Slow Cooler Size: 6-qt.
Ingredients:

- ¼ cup melted canola oil
- ¼ cup sugar
- ½ tsp. salt
- ¾ cup yellow cornmeal
- 1 cup fat-free milk
- 1 egg, lightly beaten
- 1¼ cups flour
- 4½ tsp. baking powder

Directions:

1. In mixing vessel sift together flour, cornmeal, sugar, baking powder, and salt. Make a thoroughly in the center.
2. Pour egg, milk, and oil into thoroughly. Combine into the dry mixture until just moistened.
3. Pour mixture into a oil-coated 2-qt. mould or casserole dish. Cover with a plate or lid. Place on a trivet or rack in the bottom of Crock Pot.
4. Cover. Cook on High 2–3 hours.

Exchange List Value:

- Starch 2.0
- Fat 1.0

Basic Nutritional Values:

- Calories 200 (Calories from Fat 64)
- Total Fat 7 gm (Saturated Fat 0.7 gm, Polyunsaturated Fat 2.1 gm, Monounsaturated Fat 4.0 gm)
- Cholesterol 24 mg
- Sodium 330 mg
- Total Carb 29 gm
- Dietary Fiber 1 gm
- Sugars 7 gm
- Protein 4 gm

Date and Nut Loaf

Yield: 20 servings
Preparation Time: 25 minutes
Cooking Time: 3½–4 hours
Preferred Slow Cooler Size: 6-qt.
Ingredients:

- ½ tsp. salt
- ¾ cup sugar substitute to equal ¼ cup sugar
- 1 cup walnuts, chopped
- 1 egg
- 1 Tbsp. light, soft tub margarine, melted
- 1 tsp. vanilla extract
- 1½ cups boiling water
- 1½ cups chopped dates
- 2 cups hot water
- 2 tsp. baking soda
- 2½ cups flour

Directions:

1. Pour 1½ cups boiling water over dates. Allow to stand 5–10 minutes.
2. Stir in sugar, egg, baking soda, salt, vanilla, and margarine.
3. In separate vessel, mix flour and nuts. Stir into date mixture.
4. Pour into two oil-coated 11½-oz. coffee cans or one 8-cup baking insert. If using coffee cans, cover with foil and tie. If using baking insert, cover with its lid. Place cans or insert on rack in Crock Pot. (If you don't have a rack, use rubber jar rings instead.)
5. Pour hot water around cans, up to half their height.
6. Cover Crock Pot tightly. Cook on High 3½–4 hours.

7. Take out cans or insert from cooker. Allow bread to stand in coffee cans or baking insert 10 minutes. Turn out onto cooling rack. Slice.

Exchange List Value:

- Carbohydrate 2.0
- Fat 0.5

Basic Nutritional Values:

- Calories 168 (Calories from Fat 41)
- Total Fat 5 gm (Saturated Fat 0.5 gm, Polyunsaturated Fat 3.0 gm, Monounsaturated Fat 0.8 gm)
- Cholesterol 11 mg
- Sodium 193 mg
- Total Carb 30 gm
- Dietary Fiber 2 gm
- Sugars 17 gm
- Protein 3 gm

French Bread—No Knead

Yield: 2 loaves, 19 slices per loaf, 1 slice per serving
Preparation Time: 1½ hours
Baking Time: 20 minutes
Ingredients:

- ½ cup warm water
- 1 cup boiling water
- 1 cup cold water
- 1 scant Tbsp. sugar
- 2 ¼-oz. pkgs. yeast
- 2 Tbsp. all-vegetable shortening
- 2 Tbsp. sugar
- 2 tsp. salt
- 6 cups flour

Directions:

1. Dissolve shortening, sugar, and salt in boiling water.
2. Add cold water to shortening mixture.
3. Dissolve yeast and sugar in warm water. Add to the shortening mixture.
4. Add flour. Do NOT whisk. Stir with big spoon every 10 minutes, 4 or 5 times, for about an hour.
5. Divide dough in half. Flour dough board or counter and hands and pat each section into rectangle shape Approximately ½-inch thick. Roll lengthwise in jelly roll fashion and tuck in ends. Chop slits diagonally 2–3 inches apart (shallow) on top of loaves.
6. Put on slightly oil-coated baking sheet. Allow to rise until double, Approximately 20–30 minutes depending on temperature of room.

7. Bake at 375–400°F for about 20 minutes.

Exchange List Value:

- Starch 1.0

Basic Nutritional Values:

- Calories 85 (Calories from Fat 10)
- Total Fat 1 gm (Saturated Fat 0.2 gm, Trans Fat 0.0 gm, Polyunsaturated Fat 0.3 gm, Monounsaturated Fat 0.3 gm)
- Cholesterol 0 mg
- Sodium 125 mg
- Potassium 30 gm
- Total Carb 16 gm
- Dietary Fiber 1 gm
- Sugars 1 gm
- Protein 2 gm
- Phosphorus 25 gm

Garlic Breadsticks

Yield: 26 servings, 1×9-inch breadstick per serving
Preparation Time: 10 minutes
Rising Time: 20 minutes
Baking Time: 20 minutes
Ingredients:

- ½ cup trans-fat-free tub margarine, melted
- 1 Tbsp. oil
- 1 Tbsp. sugar
- 1 Tbsp. yeast
- 1 tsp. coarsely ground salt
- 1¼ tsp. salt
- 1½ cups warm water, 110–115°F
- 1½ tsp. garlic powder
- 3 Tbsp. dried parsley flakes
- 3 Tbsp. olive oil, divided
- 3 Tbsp. Parmesan cheese
- 4 cups bread flour, also called unbleached occident flour
- Topping:

Directions:

1. Stir yeast into water in big vessel, stirring until blended.
2. Add 1 Tbsp. oil, sugar, salt and flour. Knead a little in the vessel to make sure ingredients are fully incorporated.
3. Cover with tea towel. Allow to rise 5–8 minutes in warm spot.
4. Place 1 tsp. olive oil in each of two 9×13-inch baking pans. Oil-coat pans.
5. Divide dough between baking pans. Spread to cover bottom of each pan. Set aside.
6. Prepare topping by placing melted margarine in vessel.

7. Stir in residual ingredients.
8. Pour topping mixture uniformly over 2 pans of dough.
9. Bake at 350°F for 20 minutes, or until golden brown.
10. Let cool lightly. Then using a pizza cutter, start on the 13-inch side of the pan and cut dough into 1-inch sticks.

Exchange List Value:

- Starch 1.0
- Fat 1.0

Basic Nutritional Values:

- Calories 125 (Calories from Fat 45)
- Total Fat 5 gm (Saturated Fat 0.9 gm, Trans Fat 0.0 gm, Polyunsaturated Fat 1.6 gm, Monounsaturated Fat 2.4 gm)
- Cholesterol 0 mg
- Sodium 220 mg
- Potassium 35 gm
- Total Carb 16 gm
- Dietary Fiber 1 gm
- Sugars 1 gm
- Protein 3 gm
- Phosphorus 30 gm

Garlic-Onion Bread

Yield: 12 servings, 1 slice per serving
Preparation Time: 15 minutes
Baking Time: 10 minutes
Ingredients:

- ½ Tbsp. finely chopped onion
- ½ tsp. garlic powder
- ½ tsp. salt
- 1 Tbsp. Italian seasoning
- 16-oz. loaf French bread
- 4 Tbsp. freshly grated Parmesan cheese
- 4 Tbsp. trans-fat-free tub margarine

Directions:

1. Warm margarine until softened. Stir in all residual ingredients except bread.
2. Slice bread and spread mixture thinly on each slice.
3. Warm in microwave or slow oven (200–300°F) until margarine melts instantly before serving.

Exchange List Value:

- Starch 1.5
- Fat 0.5

Basic Nutritional Values:

- Calories 140 (Calories from Fat 35)
- Total Fat 4 gm (Saturated Fat 1.0 gm, Trans Fat 0.0 gm, Polyunsaturated Fat 1.5 gm, Monounsaturated Fat 1.1 gm)
- Cholesterol 0 mg

- Sodium 345 mg
- Potassium 55 gm
- Total Carb 22 gm
- Dietary Fiber 1 gm
- Sugars 1 gm
- Protein 5 gm
- Phosphorus 55 gm

Healthy Whole Wheat Bread

Yield: 16 servings
Preparation Time: 20 minutes
Cooking Time: 2½–3 hours
Preferred Slow Cooler Size: 5- or 6-qt.
Ingredients:

- ¼ cup honey or brown sugar
- ¾ tsp. salt
- 1 pkg. active dry yeast
- 1¼ cups white flour
- 2 cups warm reconstituted fat-free powdered milk (⅔ cups powder to 1⅓ cup water)
- 2 Tbsp. canola oil
- 2½ cups whole wheat flour

Directions:

1. Combine together milk, oil, honey or brown sugar, salt, yeast, and half the flour in electric mixer vessel. Beat with mixer for 2 minutes. Add residual flour. Combine thoroughly.
2. Place dough in thoroughly -oil-coated bread or cake pan that will fit into your cooker. Cover with oil-coated tinfoil. Allow to stand for 5 minutes. Place in Crock Pot.
3. Cover cooker and bake on High 2½–3 hours. Take out pan and uncover. Allow to stand for 5 minutes. Serve warm.

Exchange List Value::

- Starch 2.0

Basic Nutritional Values:

- Calories 140 (Calories from Fat 20)
- Total Fat 2 gm (Saturated Fat 0.2 gm, Polyunsaturated Fat 0.7 gm, Monounsaturated Fat 1.1 gm)
- Cholesterol 0 mg
- Sodium 125 mg
- Total Carb 27 gm
- Dietary Fiber 3 gm
- Sugars 6 gm
- Protein 5 gm

Herbed Biscuit Knots

Yield: 20 servings
Preparation Time: 10 minutes
Baking Time: 9–12 minutes
Ingredients:

- ¼ cup canola oil
- ½ tsp. garlic powder
- ½ tsp. Italian seasoning
- ½ tsp. salt
- 12-oz. tube refrigerated buttermilk biscuits

Directions:

1. Chop each biscuit in half.
2. Roll each portion into a 6-inch-long rope.
3. Tie each in a loose knot. Place on oil-coated baking sheet.
4. Bake at 400°F for 9–12 minutes, or until golden brown.
5. While knots bake, mix oil, salt, garlic powder, and Italian seasoning in small vessel.
6. Brush over warm knots instantly after baking.

Exchange List Value:

- Starch 0.5
- Fat 1.0

Basic Nutritional Values:

- Calories 75 (Calories from Fat 45)
- Total Fat 5 gm (Saturated Fat 1.0 gm, Trans Fat 0.0 gm, Polyunsaturated Fat 1.0 gm, Monounsaturated Fat 2.7 gm)
- Cholesterol 0 mg

- Sodium 245 mg
- Potassium 25 gm
- Total Carb 7 gm
- Dietary Fiber 0 gm
- Sugars 1 gm
- Protein 1 gm
- Phosphorus 60 gm

Homemade Rolls

Yield: 20 servings, 1 roll per serving
Preparation Time: 25 minutes
Rising Time: 2 hours
Baking Time: 15–20 minutes
Ingredients:

- ¼ cup sugar
- ⅓ cup instant nonfat dry milk solids
- 1 Tbsp. salt
- 2 cups warm tap water, 120–130°F
- 2 pkgs. dry yeast
- 5 Tbsp. margarine, softened
- 5¾–6¾ cups bread flour, divided

Directions:

1. In big vessel mix 2 cups flour, dry milk, sugar, salt, and yeast. Add margarine.
2. Progressively add water to dry ingredients and whisk 2 minutes at moderate speed with a mixer. Add 1 more cup flour and whisk 2 minutes on high speed. Stir in enough flour to make a stiff dough.
3. Turn out onto a slightly floured board and knead Approximately 8–10 minutes. Place in oil-coated vessel, turning to grease top of dough.
4. Cover with a kitchen towel and let rise in warm place until doubled in bulk (about 45 minutes). Punch down and let rise again for 20 minutes.
5. Divide dough in half and cut each half into 10 equal pieces. Form into rolls and place on oil-coated baking sheet

Approximately 2 inches apart. Cover and let rise again Approximately 60 minutes.

6. Bake at 375°F for 15–20 minutes. Take out from baking sheet and brush with melted margarine.

7. Not many other people bring homemade bread or rolls to a church potluck, and I always bake them several days before the fellowship meal so I have no last-minute rush.

Exchange List Value:

- Starch 2.0
- Fat 0.5

Basic Nutritional Values:

- Calories 190 (Calories from Fat 25)
- Total Fat 3 gm (Saturated Fat 0.5 gm, Trans Fat 0.0 gm, Polyunsaturated Fat 1.2 gm, Monounsaturated Fat 0.8 gm)
- Cholesterol 0 mg
- Sodium 380 mg
- Potassium 75 gm
- Total Carb 34 gm
- Dietary Fiber 1 gm
- Sugars 4 gm
- Protein 6 gm
- Phosphorus 60 gm

Icebox Butterhorns

Yield: 36 rolls, 1 roll per serving
Preparation Time: 15 minutes
Chilling Time: 8 hours or overnight
Rising Time: 60 minutes
Baking Time: 15–20 minutes
Ingredients:

- ½ cup sugar
- ¾ cup butter-oil blend, such as Land O'Lakes tub butter with canola, at room temperature
- 1 egg
- 1 Tbsp. yeast
- 1 tsp. salt
- 2 cups fat-free milk
- 2 Tbsp. warm water, 110–115°F
- 6 cups flour

Directions:

1. Heat milk in small saucepan just until steaming.
2. Turn off the heat and let cool to 110–115°F.
3. In the meantime, in a big mixing vessel, dissolve yeast in warm water.
4. When milk has cooled, add it, plus sugar, egg, salt, and 3 cups flour to yeast mixture.
5. Beat until smooth.
6. Beat in butter spread and residual flour. The dough will be sticky.
7. Cover vessel. Refrigerate 8 hours or overnight.
8. Then divide dough into three balls.

9. Roll each ball into a 12-inch circle on slightly floured surface.
10. Chop each circle into 12 wedges each.
11. Roll up each wedge crescent-style, beginning with the wide end. Place rolls point-side down, 2 inches apart on wax paper–lined baking sheets. Curve ends, if you wish, to shape into crescents.
12. Cover and set in warm place. Allow to rise 60 minutes.
13. Bake at 350°F for 15–20 minutes.

Exchange List Value:

- Starch 1.5
- Fat 0.5

Basic Nutritional Values:

- Calories 125 (Calories from Fat 35)
- Total Fat 4 gm (Saturated Fat 1.4 gm, Trans Fat 0.0 gm, Polyunsaturated Fat 0.8 gm, Monounsaturated Fat 1.8 gm)
- Cholesterol 10 mg
- Sodium 100 mg
- Potassium 50 gm
- Total Carb 19 gm
- Dietary Fiber 1 gm
- Sugars 4 gm
- Protein 3 gm
- Phosphorus 45 gm

Lemon Bread

Yield: 12 servings
Preparation Time: 20 minutes
Cooking Time: 2–2¼ hours
Preferred Slow Cooker Size: 4-qt.
Ingredients:

- ¼ cup canola oil
- ½ cup fat-free milk
- ½ tsp. salt
- 1⅔ cups flour
- 1⅔ tsp. baking powder
- 2 eggs, beaten
- 4 oz. chopped walnuts
- 6 Tbsp. sugar substitute to equal 3 Tbsp. sugar
- grated peel from 1 lemon

Glaze:

- ¼ cup powdered sugar
- juice of 1 lemon

Directions:

1. Cream together oil and sugar. Add eggs. Combine thoroughly.
2. Sift together flour, baking powder, and salt. Add flour mixture and milk alternately to shortening mixture.
3. Stir in nuts and lemon peel.
4. Spoon batter into thoroughly -oil-coated 2-lb. coffee can or 9×5-inch loaf pan and cover with thoroughly -oil-coated foil. Place in cooker set on High for 2–2¼ hours, or until done. Take out bread from coffee can or pan.

5. For glaze: Combine together powdered sugar and lemon juice. Pour over loaf.

Exchange List Value:

- Starch 1.5
- Fat 1.0

Basic Nutritional Values:

- Calories 176 (Calories from Fat 66)
- Total Fat 7 gm (Saturated Fat 0.9 gm, Polyunsaturated Fat 2.7 gm, Monounsaturated Fat 3.3 gm)
- Cholesterol 37 mg
- Sodium 168 mg
- Total Carb 24 gm
- Dietary Fiber 1 gm
- Sugars 10 gm

Oatmeal Herb Bread

Yield: 1 loaf, 16 slices in the loaf, 1 slice per serving
Preparation Time: 20 minutes
Rising Time: 65–85 minutes
Baking Time: 30–35 minutes
Standing Time: 30–45 minutes
Ingredients:

- ½ cup dry quick oats
- 1 cup warm water (110–115°F)
- 1 egg, slightly beaten
- 1 Tbsp. yeast
- 1 tsp. dried basil
- 1 tsp. dried oregano
- 1 tsp. dried parsley
- 1 tsp. dried sage
- 1 tsp. dried thyme
- 1 tsp. salt
- 2 Tbsp. brown sugar
- 3 Tbsp. olive oil
- 3½–4 cups unbleached bread flour, also called occident flour

Directions:

1. Dissolve sugar in warm water in a big mixing vessel.
2. Drizzle yeast over top.
3. Allow torest 5–10 minutes until yeast begins to foam.
4. Stir in egg, olive oil, salt, oats, and herbs.
5. Progressively add in flour, one cup at a time, mixing until a ball forms that is not too dense. Dough should be soft but not sticky.
6. Knead Approximately 5 minutes on floured surface.

7. Oil-coat a big vessel. Place dough in vessel and cover with a tea towel.
8. Place in warm spot. Allow to rise until doubled, Approximately 30–45 minutes.
9. Punch down. Form into a loaf.
10. Place in oil-coated loaf pan. Allow to rise until dough comes to top of pan, Approximately 35–40 minutes.
11. In the meantime, preheat oven to 350°F. Place risen loaf in oven. Bake about 30–35 minutes. Loaf should be golden brown and should sound hollow when tapped.
12. Cool 10 minutes before taking out of pan.
13. Allow to cool until lukewarm before slicing to keep moisture in the loaf. Slice the loaf just before serving.

Exchange List Value:

- Starch 2.0
- Fat 0.5

Basic Nutritional Values:

- Calories 175 (Calories from Fat 45)
- Total Fat 5 gm (Saturated Fat 1.0 gm, Trans Fat 0.0 gm, Polyunsaturated Fat 0.9 gm, Monounsaturated Fat 2.7 gm)
- Cholesterol 70 mg
- Sodium 175 mg
- Potassium 85 gm
- Total Carb 26 gm
- Dietary Fiber 1 gm
- Sugars 2 gm
- Protein 7 gm
- Phosphorus 85 gm

Old-Fashioned Gingerbread Loaf

Yield: 16 servings
Preparation Time: 25 minutes
Cooking Time: 2½–3 hours
Preferred Slow Cooker Size: 4-qt.
Ingredients:

- ½ tsp. ground cloves
- ½ tsp. salt
- 1 cup hot water
- 1 cup light molasses
- 1 egg
- 1 tsp. ground cinnamon
- 1½ tsp. baking soda
- 2 tsp. ground ginger
- 2½ cups flour
- 4 Tbsp. margarine, softened
- 4 Tbsp. sugar substitute to equal 2 Tbsp. sugar
- nutmeg, optional
- warm applesauce, optional
- whipped cream, optional

Directions:

1. Cream together margarine and sugar substitute. Add egg and molasses. Combine thoroughly.
2. Stir in flour, baking soda, cinnamon, ginger, cloves, and salt. Combine thoroughly.
3. Add hot water. Beat thoroughly.
4. Pour batter into oil-coated and floured 2-lb. coffee can.
5. Place can in cooker. Cover top of can with 8 paper towels. Cover cooker and bake on High 2½–3 hours.

6. Serve with applesauce, if desired. Top with whipped cream and sprinkle with nutmeg, if using.

Exchange List Value:

- Carbohydrate 2.0
- Fat 0.5

Basic Nutritional Values:

- Calories 168 (Calories from Fat 30)
- Total Fat 3 gm (Saturated Fat 0.7 gm, Polyunsaturated Fat 1.0 gm, Monounsaturated Fat 1.4 gm)
- Cholesterol 13 mg
- Sodium 235 mg
- Total Carb 32 gm
- Dietary Fiber 1 gm
- Sugars 16 gm
- Protein 2 gm

Pumpernickel Bread

Yield: 4 loaves, 16 slices per loaf, 1 slice per serving
Preparation Time: 35 minutes
Rising Time: 2 ¼ hours
Cooking/Baking Time: 60 minutes
Ingredients:

- ½ cup dark molasses
- ½ cup flax
- ½ cup millet, optional
- ¾ cup yellow cornmeal
- 1 cup bran
- 1 cup warm water
- 1 Tbsp. trans-fat-free tub margarine
- 1 Tbsp. unsweetened cocoa, optional
- 1 tsp. salt
- 2 cups mashed potatoes
- 2 tsp. caraway seeds
- 2 tsp. sugar
- 3 Tbsp. yeast
- 3¼ cups water
- 3½ cups rye flour
- 3½ cups whole wheat flour
- 4½ cups white flour

Directions:

1. Dissolve yeast with sugar in 1 cup warm water. Allow to stand 10 minutes until bubbly. Stir thoroughly.
2. Mix 3¼ cups water, molasses, and margarine in saucepan. Heat over low heat until margarine is blended. When room temperature, add salt and yeast mixture.
3. Mix all flours and cocoa (if using) in big vessel.

4. Add bran, cornmeal, millet (if using), and mashed potatoes. Add to liquid yeast mixture and whisk until completely combined. Stir in caraway seeds and flax and mix thoroughly.
5. Allow dough to rest 15 minutes. Knead until smooth.
6. Allow to rise until double in bulk, Approximately 60 minutes.
7. Punch down. Allow to rise again for approximately half an hour.
8. Divide into 4 pieces and shape into loaves or balls and place in oil-coated tins.
9. Cover and let rise in warm place, Approximately 45 minutes.
10. Bake at 325°F for 45–50 minutes or until done.

Exchange List Value:

- Starch 1.5

Basic Nutritional Values:

- Calories 105 (Calories from Fat 15)
- Total Fat 2 gm (Saturated Fat 0.2 gm, Trans Fat 0.0 gm, Polyunsaturated Fat 0.5 gm, Monounsaturated Fat 0.3 gm)
- Cholesterol 0 mg
- Sodium 60 mg
- Potassium 170 gm
- Total Carb 22 gm
- Dietary Fiber 4 gm
- Sugars 2 gm
- Protein 4 gm
- Phosphorus 100 gm

Pumpkin Bread

Yield: 2 big loaves, or 8 small loaves, 32 slices total, 1 slice per serving
Preparation Time: 15–20 minutes
Baking Time: 25–70 minutes, depending on size of loaves
Cooling Time: 40 minutes
Ingredients:

- ½ tsp. baking powder
- ½ tsp. cloves
- ½ tsp. nutmeg
- ⅔ cup chopped nuts
- ⅔ cup cooking oil
- ⅔ cup water
- 1 cup raisins
- 1 tsp. cinnamon
- 1 tsp. salt
- 1⅓ cup Splenda Sugar Blend
- 16-oz. can pumpkin
- 2 tsp. baking soda
- 3⅓ cups flour
- 4 eggs

Directions:

1. In big vessel, cream oil and Splenda until fluffy.
2. Blend in eggs, and then pumpkin and water.
3. In a separate vessel, sift together flour, baking soda, salt, baking powder, cinnamon, cloves, and nutmeg.
4. Stir sifted dry ingredients into pumpkin mixture.
5. Stir in raisins and nuts.
6. Pour into two oil-coated 5×9-inch loaf pans or eight 3×6-inch loaf pans. Bake at 350°F for 60–70 minutes for big

loaves; 25–30 minutes for small loaves. Test that bread is done by inserting toothpick into center of loaves. If pick comes out unsoiled, bread is finished baking. If it doesn't, continue baking 3–5 minutes more. Test again.
7. Let cool in pans 10 minutes. Take out from pan and let cool another approximately half an hour or so before slicing and serving.

Exchange List Value:

- Carbohydrate 1.5
- Fat 0.5

Basic Nutritional Values:

- Calories 125 (Calories from Fat 20)
- Total Fat 2.5 gm (Saturated Fat 0.4 gm, Trans Fat 0.0 gm, Polyunsaturated Fat 1.4 gm, Monounsaturated Fat 0.7 gm)
- Cholesterol 25 mg
- Sodium 170 mg
- Potassium 95 gm
- Total Carb 23 gm
- Dietary Fiber 1 gm
- Sugars 11 gm
- Protein 3 gm
- Phosphorus 50 gm

Whole Wheat Rolls

Yield: 2 dozen rolls, 1 roll per serving
Preparation Time: 25 minutes
Cooling Time: 20 minutes
Rising Time: Approximately 2 hours
Baking Time: 20 minutes
Ingredients:

- ¼ cup sugar
- ½ cup warm water
- 1 Tbsp. salt
- 1 tsp. sugar
- 1¾ cups fat-free milk, scalded
- 2 cups whole wheat flour
- 2 pkgs. dry yeast
- 3 cups white flour, or more if needed
- 3 egg whites
- 3 Tbsp. all-vegetable shortening

Directions:

1. Mix yeast and warm water in small vessel. Drizzle 1 tsp. sugar over yeast and water. Set aside.
2. Pour scalded milk over ¼ cup sugar, salt, and shortening in big vessel. Cool until lukewarm. Add yeast mixture and stir thoroughly.
3. Add whole wheat flour and egg whites. Beat thoroughly and gradually add white flour until you have soft dough.
4. Turn onto floured surface and knead until dough is elastic, Approximately 5–7 minutes. Place in oil-coated vessel, turning dough to grease top. Cover with clean cloth and let rise until doubled in bulk.

5. Punch down and shape into rolls. Place on oil-coated cookie sheets until double.
6. Bake at 350° for 20 minutes or until slightly browned.

Exchange List Value:

- Starch 1.5

Basic Nutritional Values:

- Calories 125 (Calories from Fat 20)
- Total Fat 2 gm (Saturated Fat 0.4 gm, Trans Fat 0.0 gm, Polyunsaturated Fat 0.6 gm, Monounsaturated Fat 0.7 gm)
- Cholesterol 0 mg
- Sodium 305 mg
- Potassium 105 gm
- Total Carb 23 gm
- Dietary Fiber 2 gm
- Sugars 3 gm
- Protein 4 gm
- Phosphorus 80 gm

Zucchini Bread

Yield: 2 big loaves, or 7 small loaves, 30 slices total, 1 slice per serving
Preparation Time: 20–30 minutes
Baking Time: 20–45 minutes
Ingredients:

- ½ cup dry quick, or old-fashioned, oats
- ½ tsp. nutmeg
- ⅔ cup canola oil
- 1 cup brown sugar
- 1 tsp. baking powder
- 1 tsp. baking soda
- 1 tsp. salt
- 1 tsp. vanilla extract
- 1½ cups flour
- 1½ cups shredded zucchini
- 1½ tsp. cinnamon
- 2 cups finely chopped walnuts
- 3 eggs
- 4 oz. fat-free cream cheese, cut in chunks
- 4 oz. Neufchâtel (⅓-less-fat) cream cheese, cut in chunks

Directions:

1. In an electric mixer vessel, whisk eggs, sugar, oil, and vanilla 3 minutes.
2. Add cream cheese and whisk 1 minute.
3. Combine flour, oats, baking powder, baking soda, cinnamon, nutmeg, and salt in another vessel.
4. Fold lightly into egg mixture.
5. Fold in zucchini and nuts.

6. Pour into two x-inch oil-coated loaf pans. Bake at 350°F for 45 minutes. Or divide among seven small loaf pans, and then bake at 350°F for 20 minutes. Test that loaves are finished by inserting toothpick into center of loaves. If pick comes out unsoiled, baking is complete. If not, bake another 3–5 minutes and test again with toothpick.

Exchange List Value:

- Carbohydrate 1.0
- Fat 2.0

Basic Nutritional Values:

- Calories 165 (Calories from Fat 110)
- Total Fat 12 gm (Saturated Fat 1.5 gm, Trans Fat 0.0 gm, Polyunsaturated Fat 5.3 gm, Monounsaturated Fat 4.2 gm)
- Cholesterol 20 mg
- Sodium 180 mg
- Potassium 90 gm
- Total Carb 12 gm
- Dietary Fiber 1 gm
- Sugars 5 gm
- Protein 4 gm
- Phosphorus 95 gm

Bonus: Diabetic Appetizers

Appetizers are the heart of a meal course. Even if you're a diabetic, you can enjoy insanely delicious appetizers, as long as you can control yourself and can bring yourself to stop once your allowed limits are met.

So, the next time you're planning a meal, don't be afraid of adding appetizers to them! Diabetes or not, good food is a pleasure that absolutely cannot be missed. The appetizer recipes in this book are designed keeping diabetics in mind, but just remember that excess of everything is bad. Diabetics can indulge in these appetizer recipes, but overeating them is still not a good idea.

So, what are we waiting for? Let's dive right into the recipes!

Apricot-Glazed Wings

Yield: 8–10 servings
Preparation Time: 30 minutes
Broiling Time: 16 minutes
Chilling Time: 4–6 hours
Ideal slow-cooker size: 3-qt.
Ingredients:

- ¼ cup honey Catalina dressing
- 1 small onion, minced
- 1 tsp. lime juice
- 12-oz. jar no sugar added or sugar-free apricot preserves
- 2 Tbsp. barbecue sauce
- 2 Tbsp. honey mustard
- 4 dashes hot sauce
- 4 lbs. chicken wings, cut at the joint, tips removed and discarded
- garlic powder, to taste
- pepper, to taste
- salt, to taste

Directions:

1. Preheat your oven to a low broil.
2. Place your wing pieces on a baking sheet and drizzle both sides with salt, pepper, and garlic powder. Place them under the broiler for approximately 8 minutes on each side.
3. As the wings broil, combine together the apricot preserves, honey Catalina dressing, honey mustard, barbecue sauce, lime juice, hot sauce, and onion.
4. When your wings are done under the broiler, Put them into a greased slow cooker.
5. Pour the sauce you just mixed over the top, toss the wings around using tongs to make sure they are covered completely with the sauce.

6. Cook on Low for approximately 4–6 hours.

Exchange List Value:

- Fruit 1.0
- Med-Fat Meat 4.0

Basic Nutritional Values:

- Calories 417 (Calories from Fat 180)
- Total Fat 20 gm (Saturated Fat 5.4 gm, Trans Fat 0.5 gm, Polyunsaturated Fat 3.6 gm, Monounsaturated Fat 8.5 gm)
- Cholesterol 82 mg
- Sodium 589 mg
- Potassium 449 gm
- Total Carb 24 gm
- Dietary Fiber 1 gm
- Sugars 20.3gm
- Protein 31.2 gm
- Phosphorus 230 gm

Baked Brie

Yield: 60 servings, 1 Tbsp. per serving
Preparation Time: 15 minutes
Baking Time: 20–25 minutes
Ingredients:

- ¼ cup amaretto
- ½ cup chopped pecans
- ½ cup Splenda Brown Sugar Blend
- ¾ cup dried cherries
- 16-oz. round Brie

Directions:

1. Put Brie in round oven-safe casserole or pie plate.
2. Combine brown sugar and amaretto together; spread on top of cheese.
3. Drizzle with pecans and cherries.
4. Bake at 375°F for approximately 20–25 minutes.

Serving suggestion:

- Serve with French bread slices.
- You can use Grand Marnier or a hazelnut liqueur too if you wish. You can also use macadamia nuts or filberts in place of pecans.

Exchange List Value:

- Fat 1.0

Basic Nutritional Values:

- Calories 45 (Calories from Fat 20)
- Total Fat 2.5 gm (Saturated Fat 1.3 gm, Trans Fat 0.0 gm, Polyunsaturated Fat 0.2 gm, Monounsaturated Fat 1.0 gm)
- Cholesterol 5 mg
- Sodium 55 mg
- Potassium 25 gm
- Total Carb 4 gm
- Dietary Fiber 0 gm
- Sugars 2 gm

- Protein 1 gm
- Phosphorus 25 gm

Baked Brie with Cranberry Chutney

Yield: 25 servings
Preparation Time: 25 minutes
Chilling Time: 4½ hours
Ideal slow-cooker size: 1-qt.
Ingredients:

- ⅛ tsp. ground cloves
- ¼ tsp. cinnamon
- ⅓ cup cider vinegar
- ½ cup brown sugar
- 1 cup fresh, or dried, cranberries
- 1 Tbsp. sliced almonds, toasted
- 2 Tbsp. water or orange juice
- 2 tsp. minced crystallized ginger
- 8-oz. round of Brie cheese
- crackers
- oil

Directions:

1. Combine together cranberries, brown sugar, vinegar, water or juice, ginger, cinnamon, and cloves in Crock pot.
2. Cover. Cook on Low heat for about 4 hours. Mix once near the end to see if it is thickening. If not, take off the top, increase the heat to High, and cook for half an hour without cover.
3. Pour cranberry chutney in covered container and chill for up to 2 weeks. When ready to serve, allow to come to room temperature.
4. Line a shallow baking dish or ovenproof plate with vegetable oil; place Brie, still in rind, on plate.
5. Bake uncovered at 350°F for 9 minutes, until cheese is soft and partially melted. Take out of oven.
6. Pour half the chutney and garnish with almonds on top and serve with crackers.

Exchange List Value:
- Fat 1.0

Basic Nutritional Values:
- Calories 38 (Calories from Fat 23)
- Total Fat 3 gm (Saturated Fat 1.5 gm, Polyunsaturated Fat 0.1 gm, Monounsaturated Fat 0.8 gm)
- Cholesterol 8 mg
- Sodium 67 mg
- Total Carb 3 gm
- Dietary Fiber 0 gm
- Sugars 3 gm
- Protein 1 gm

Basic Deviled Eggs

Ingredients:

- ⅛ tsp. salt
- ¼ cup light mayonnaise
- 1 tsp. prepared mustard
- 1 tsp. vinegar
- 6 big eggs, hard-boiled and peeled
- paprika
- parsley sprigs, for garnish
- sprinkle of pepper

Directions:

To hard-boil eggs:

1. Put eggs in a single layer in a lidded pan.
2. Pour cold water into the pan until the eggs are covered completely.
3. Cover the pan and bring to a full broil.
4. Just as the water begins the full boil, instantly turn the heat down to low for a simmer. Let it barely simmer for exactly 18 minutes.
5. Turn off the heat, eliminate the hot water, and pour in cold water to cool the eggs.

To make deviled eggs:

1. Slice the eggs in half lengthwise. Carefully take out the yolk sections into a vessel.
2. Eliminate two yolks if using a recipe for 6; Eliminate 4 yolks if using a recipe for 12. Mash the rest of the yolk sections together using a fork. Mix in the rest of the ingredients with yolk mixture until smooth.
3. Fill the vacant egg whites. The filling will look like a little mound in the egg white. Garnish, if you wish.
4. Refrigerate.

Exchange List Value:

• Med-Fat Meat 1.0

Basic Nutritional Values:

- Calories 75 (Calories from Fat 55)
- Total Fat 6 gm (Saturated Fat 1.4 gm, Trans Fat 0.0 gm, Polyunsaturated Fat 2.0 gm, Monounsaturated Fat 1.9 gm)
- Cholesterol 125 mg
- Sodium 205 mg
- Potassium 70 gm
- Total Carb 1 gm
- Dietary Fiber 0 gm
- Sugars 1 gm
- Protein 6 gm
- Phosphorus 70 gm

Buffalo Chicken Dip

Yield: 26 servings, ¼ cup per serving
Preparation Time: 15 minutes
Chilling Time: 20–60 minutes
Ingredients:

- ¾ cup Frank's RedHot Original Cayenne Pepper Sauce
- 1 cup light ranch dressing
- 10-oz. can chunk chicken, drained
- 1½ cups shredded cheddar Jack cheese, divided
- 2 8-oz. pkgs. fat-free cream cheese, softened
- tortilla chips

Directions:

1. Heat chicken and hot sauce in a big frying pan over medium heat until heated thoroughly.
2. Mix in cream cheese and ranch dressing. Cook, stirring, until well blended and warm.
3. Combine in half of shredded cheese.
4. Move the mixture to a small slow cooker. Sprinkle the remaining cheese over the top.
5. Cover and cook on Low setting until hot and bubbly. Serve with tortilla chips.

Exchange List Values:

- Lean Meat 1.0
- Fat 0.5

Basic Nutritional Values:

- Calories 75 (Calories from Fat 35)
- Total Fat 4 gm (Saturated Fat 1.1 gm, Trans Fat 0.0 gm, Polyunsaturated Fat 0.8 gm, Monounsaturated Fat 0.9 gm)
- Cholesterol 15 mg
- Sodium 475 mg
- Potassium 90 gm
- Total Carb 2 gm
- Dietary Fiber 0 gm

- Sugars 1 gm
- Protein 6 gm
- Phosphorus 160 gm

Cheese and Olive Spread

Yield: 2 cups, 1 Tbsp. per serving
Preparation Time: 15 minutes
Chilling Time: 1 hour
Ingredients:

- ¼ cup green onions, chopped
- ¼ cup stuffed green olives, chopped
- ¼ tsp. ground red pepper, or to taste
- ½ cup light mayonnaise
- 2 Tbsp. lemon juice
- 4 oz. fat-free cream cheese, softened
- 4 oz. Neufchâtel (⅓-less-fat) cream cheese, softened
- 8-oz. pkg. reduced-fat shredded mild cheddar cheese

Directions:

1. Combine the ingredients.
2. Refrigerate for at least 60 minutes.

Serving suggestion:
Serve with Ritz crackers.
Exchange List Value:

- Fat 1.0

Basic Nutritional Values:

- Calories 45 (Calories from Fat 30)
- Total Fat 4 gm (Saturated Fat 1.5 gm, Trans Fat 0.0 gm, Polyunsaturated Fat 0.6 gm, Monounsaturated Fat 0.9 gm)
- Cholesterol 10 mg
- Sodium 145 mg
- Potassium 25 gm
- Total Carb 1 gm
- Dietary Fiber 0 gm
- Sugars 0 gm
- Protein 3 gm
- Phosphorus 65 gm

Cheesy Chorizo Dip

Yield: approximately 8 servings, ¼ cup per person
Preparation Time: 15 minutes
Chilling Time: 2 hours
Ideal slow-cooker size: 1½–2-qt.
Ingredients:

- 12 oz. Velveeta cheese
- 8 oz. chorizo, browned
- ½ cup salsa

Directions:

1. Line the slow cooker with non-stick spray.
2. Put the Velveeta cheese in the show cooker and place the chorizo and salsa over it.
3. Cover and cook on Low heat for 2 hours, or until all is melted. Turn to warm. Serve.

Exchange List Value:

- Med-Fat Meat 0.5
- Fat 0.5
- Milk 0.5

Basic Nutritional Values:

- Calories 135 (Calories from Fat 82) Total Fat 9 gm (Saturated Fat 5.2 gm, Trans Fat 0 gm, Polyunsaturated Fat 0.5 gm, Monounsaturated Fat 2.0 gm)
- Cholesterol 15 mg
- Sodium 581 mg
- Potassium 166 gm
- Total Carb 3.6 gm
- Dietary Fiber 0.2 gm
- Sugars 2.9gm
- Protein 7.4 gm
- Phosphorus 242 gm

Cheesy Hot Bean Dip

Yield: 20 servings
Preparation Time: 10 minutes
Chilling Time: 2 hours
Ideal slow-cooker size: 3-qt.
Ingredients:
- ¼ tsp. ground cumin
- 1 cup fat-free sour cream
- 1 cup reduced-fat Cheddar cheese
- 1 cup salsa
- 1 cup shredded reduced-fat Monterey Jack
- 1 Tbsp. chili powder
- 16-oz. can refried beans
- 3-oz. pkg. fat-free cream cheese, cubed

Directions:
1. Mix all ingredients in slow cooker.
2. Cover. Cook on High 2 hours. Whisk 2–3 times during cooking.

Serving suggestion:
Serve warm from the cooker with tortilla chips.
Exchange List Values:
- Carbohydrate 0.5
- Fat 0.5

Basic Nutritional Values:
- Calories 65 (Calories from Fat 22)
- Total Fat 2 gm (Saturated Fat 1.5 gm, Polyunsaturated Fat 0.1 gm, Monounsaturated Fat 0.7 gm)
- Cholesterol 11 mg
- Sodium 275 mg
- Total Carb 6 gm
- Dietary Fiber 1 gm
- Sugars 2 gm
- Protein 6 gm

Cheesy New Orleans Shrimp Dip

Yield: 20 servings
Preparation Time: 25 minutes
Chilling Time: 1 hour
Ideal slow-cooker size: 1-qt.
Ingredients:

- ⅛ tsp. cayenne pepper
- 1 clove garlic, minced
- 1 medium tomato, peeled and chopped
- 1 slice bacon
- 3 medium onions, chopped
- 4 drops Tabasco sauce
- 4 jumbo shrimp, peeled and deveined
- 7 oz. reduced-fat Monterey Jack cheese, shredded
- chips
- dash black pepper
- milk to thin dip, optional

Directions:

1. Cook bacon until crunchy. Drain using paper towel. Crumble.
2. Brown the onions and garlic in skillet sprayed with non-fat cooking spray. Drain using paper towel.
3. Crudely chop shrimp.
4. Mix all ingredients except chips, and place in slow cooker.
5. Cover. Cook on Low for 60 minutes, or until cheese is liquefied. Thin with milk if too dense.
6. Serve with chips.

Exchange List Value:

- Lean Meat 1.0

Basic Nutritional Values:

- Calories 43 (Calories from Fat 18)
- Total Fat 2 gm (Saturated Fat 1.5 gm, Polyunsaturated Fat 0.1 gm, Monounsaturated Fat 0.6 gm)

- Cholesterol 13 mg
- Sodium 90 mg
- Total Carb 2 gm
- Dietary Fiber 0 gm
- Sugars 2 gm
- Protein 4 gm

Chicken Salad Spread

Yield: 8 servings, approximately ¼ cup per serving
Preparation Time: 20 minutes
Ingredients:

- ½ cup reduced-fat light mayonnaise
- ½ tsp. cream-style horseradish
- ½ tsp. prepared mustard
- ½ tsp. salt
- ½ tsp. Worcestershire sauce
- 1 Tbsp. finely chopped celery
- 1 Tbsp. finely chopped onion
- 1 tsp. white sugar
- 2 cups shredded, cooked chicken

Directions:

1. Ready the cooked chicken by eliminating all skin, bones, and tendons. Save broth and pieces of chicken. Shred chicken chunks using a blender. Set aside and allow it to cool to room temperature compeltely.
2. Mix all other ingredients.
3. Put the cooled, shredded chicken into mayonnaise mixture. If the mixture is too dense to spread easily, Put in minuscule amounts of chicken broth until it spreads with ease.

Serving suggestion:
Spread filling generously between bread or rolls.
Exchange List Value:

- Lean Meat 2.0
- Fat 0.5

Basic Nutritional Values:

- Calories 105 (Calories from Fat 55)
- Total Fat 6 gm (Saturated Fat 1.2 gm, Trans Fat 0.0 gm, Polyunsaturated Fat 2.6 gm, Monounsaturated Fat 1.9 gm)
- Cholesterol 35 mg

- Sodium 310 mg
- Potassium 100 gm
- Total Carb 2 gm
- Dietary Fiber 0 gm
- Sugars 1 gm
- Protein 10 gm
- Phosphorus 75 gm

Creamy Caramel Dip

Yield: 40 servings, 1 Tbsp. per serving
Preparation Time: 20 minutes
Chilling Time: 1 hour
Ingredients:

- ¾ cup brown sugar
- 1 cup fat-free milk
- 1 cup fat-free sour cream
- 2 tsp. vanilla extract
- 3.4-oz. pkg. instant vanilla pudding mix
- 8-oz. fat-free cream cheese, softened

Directions:

1. Blend cream cheese and brown sugar.
2. Put in the sour cream, vanilla, milk, and pudding mix. Mis thoroughly.
3. Chill for minimum 60 minutes.

Serving suggestion:
Serve as a dip for pineapples, apples, grapes, strawberries, etc.
Exchange List Value:

- Carbohydrate 0.5

Basic Nutritional Values:

- Calories 30 (Calories from Fat 0)
- Total Fat 0 gm (Saturated Fat 0.0 gm, Trans Fat 0.0 gm, Polyunsaturated Fat 0.0 gm, Monounsaturated Fat 0.0 gm)
- Cholesterol 0 mg
- Sodium 80 mg
- Potassium 40 gm
- Total Carb 7 gm
- Dietary Fiber 0 gm
- Sugars 5 gm
- Protein 1 gm
- Phosphorus 60 gm

Dill Pickle Eggs

Ingredients:

- ⅛ tsp. pepper
- ¼ cup fat-free plain yogurt or light mayonnaise
- ¼ tsp. salt
- ¼ tsp. Worcestershire sauce
- 1 Tbsp. pickle relish
- 1 tsp. dill weed
- 1 tsp. prepared mustard
- 1 tsp. vinegar
- 6 big eggs, hard-boiled and peeled
- paprika
- pickle slice, to garnish

Directions:

To hard-boil eggs:

1. Put eggs in a single layer in a lidded pan.
2. Pour cold water into the pan until the eggs are covered completely.
3. Cover the pan and bring to a full broil.
4. Just as the water begins the full boil, instantly turn the heat down to low for a simmer. Let it barely simmer for exactly 18 minutes.
5. Turn off the heat, eliminate the hot water, and pour in cold water to cool the eggs.

To make deviled eggs:

1. Slice the eggs in half lengthwise. Carefully take out the yolk sections into a vessel.
2. Eliminate two yolks if using a recipe for 6; Eliminate 4 yolks if using a recipe for 12. Mash the rest of the yolk sections together using a fork. Mix in the rest of the ingredients with yolk mixture until smooth.
3. Fill the vacant egg whites. The filling will look like a little mound in the egg white. Garnish, if you wish.

4. Refrigerate.

Exchange List Value:
• Med-Fat Meat 1.0
Basic Nutritional Values:
- Calories 65 (Calories from Fat 30)
- Total Fat 4 gm (Saturated Fat 1.1 gm, Trans Fat 0.0 gm, Polyunsaturated Fat 0.6 gm, Monounsaturated Fat 1.3 gm)
- Cholesterol 125 mg
- Sodium 205 mg
- Potassium 95 gm
- Total Carb 2 gm
- Dietary Fiber 0 gm
- Sugars 2 gm
- Protein 6 gm
- Phosphorus 85 gm

Easy Layered Taco Dip

Yield: 10 servings
Preparation Time: 15 minutes

Ingredients:
- 1 cup chopped tomato
- 1 cup reduced-fat shredded Mexi-blend cheesetortilla chips
- 4 cups shredded lettuce
- 8-oz. fat-free cream cheese, softened
- 8-oz. fat-free sour cream
- 8-oz. taco sauce or salsa
- chopped green pepper, optional

Directions:
1. If possible, put in the lettuce, tomato and cheese at the last minute so the lettuce doesn't get mushy.
2. Omit salsa and lettuce. Put 3 Tbsp. taco seasoning into the sour cream and cream cheese and sprinkle with a layer of chopped onion.
3. Whisk the cream cheese and sour cream until smooth. Spread in bottom of a 9x13-inch dish.
4. Cover the sour cream mixture with taco, then add layers of lettuce, tomato, pepper (if using), and cheese.
5. Serve with tortilla chips.

Exchange List Value:
- Carbohydrate 0.5
- Lean Meat 1.0

Basic Nutritional Values:
- Calories 90 (Calories from Fat 20)
- Total Fat 2.5 gm (Saturated Fat 1.5 gm, Trans Fat 0.0 gm, Polyunsaturated Fat 0.1 gm, Monounsaturated Fat 0.6 gm)
- Cholesterol 10 mg
- Sodium 415 mg

- Potassium 175 gm
- Total Carb 9 gm
- Dietary Fiber 1 gm
- Sugars 3 gm
- Protein 7 gm
- Phosphorus 205 gm

Easy Turkey Roll-Ups

Yield: 6 servings, 2 roll-ups per serving

Preparation Time: 10 minutes

Ingredients:

- ¾ cup shredded lettuce
- 12 slices deli shaved 97%-fat-free turkey breast, 6 oz. total
- 3 6-inch flour tortillas
- 3 Tbsp. chive and onion cream cheese

Directions:

1. Coat the top of the tortillas with cream cheese. Place the turkey on top. Place lettuce on bottom halves of tortillas; roll up.
2. Cut each into 4 pieces and place flat to serve.

Exchange List Value:

- Starch 0.5
- Lean Meat 1.0

Basic Nutritional Values:

- Calories 90 (Calories from Fat 20)
- Total Fat 2.5 gm (Saturated Fat 1.1 gm, Trans Fat 0.0 gm, Polyunsaturated Fat 0.5 gm, Monounsaturated Fat 0.8 gm)
- Cholesterol 15 mg
- Sodium 365 mg
- Potassium 125 gm
- Total Carb 8 gm
- Dietary Fiber 1 gm
- Sugars 1 gm
- Protein 9 gm
- Phosphorus 95 gm

Fruit and Nut Spread

Yield: 24 servings, 1 Tbsp. per serving
Preparation Time: 15 minutes
Chilling Time: 30 minutes
Ingredients:

- ¼ cup orange juice
- ½ cup dried cranberries
- ½ cup pecans, chopped
- 8-oz. Neufchâtel (⅓-less-fat) cream cheese, softened

Directions:

1. In a small mixing vessel, whisk cream cheese and orange juice until smooth.
2. Fold in cranberries and pecans.
3. Cover and place in the refrigerator for about 30 minutes.

Good Side Dishes With This Recipe:

Good with crackers or spread on bagels

Exchange List Value:

- Fat 1.0

Basic Nutritional Values:

- Calories 50 (Calories from Fat 35)
- Total Fat 4 gm (Saturated Fat 1.4 gm, Trans Fat 0.0 gm, Polyunsaturated Fat 0.6 gm, Monounsaturated Fat 1.5 gm)
- Cholesterol 5 mg
- Sodium 40 mg
- Potassium 30 gm
- Total Carb 3 gm
- Dietary Fiber 0 gm
- Sugars 2 gm
- Protein 1 gm
- Phosphorus 20 gm

Fruit Dip

Yield: 10 servings, 2 Tbsp. per serving
Preparation Time: 10 minutes
Ingredients:
- 1 cup fat-free sour cream
- 2 Tbsp. brown sugar
- ½ tsp. cinnamon
- ¼ tsp. vanilla extract

Directions:
1. Combine ingredients together.
2. Serve with cut-up apples, grapes, and bananas (not included in nutritional info).

Exchange List Value: (not including fruit)
- Carbohydrate 0.5

Basic Nutritional Values: (not including fruit)
- Calories 30 (Calories from Fat 0)
- Total Fat 0 gm (Saturated Fat 0.1 gm, Trans Fat 0.0 gm, Polyunsaturated Fat 0.0 gm, Monounsaturated Fat 0.0 gm)
- Cholesterol 0 mg
- Sodium 30 mg
- Potassium 35 gm
- Total Carb 7 gm
- Dietary Fiber 0 gm
- Sugars 4 gm
- Protein 1 gm
- Phosphorus 25 gm

Fruit Salsa with Cinnamon Chips

Yield: 12 servings, 6 chips and approximately ⅓ cup salsa per serving
Preparation Time: 45 minutes
Baking Time: 12 minutes
Ingredients:

Cinnamon Chips:
- ¾ tsp. cinnamon
- 2 Tbsp. sugar
- 6 6-inch flour tortillas
- butter flavor cooking spray

Salsa:
- ¼ cup orange juice
- ¼ tsp. nutmeg
- ¼–½ tsp. cinnamon
- ½ cup blueberries
- 1 apple, chopped
- 1 cup chopped strawberries
- 1 kiwi, peeled and chopped
- 1 orange, peeled and chopped
- 2 Tbsp. honey
- 2 Tbsp. sugar-free jam (any flavor)
- pinch salt

Directions:

1. To prepare the cinnamon chips, chop the tortillas into 12 wedges and place on a baking sheet. Lightly sprinkle with cooking spray.
2. Combine cinnamon and sugar together.
3. Drizzle tortilla wedges with the cinnamon sugar.
4. Bake for 10 minutes at 350°F, then broil for 2 minutes. Take out of pan until cool.
5. To make salsa, toss all prepared fruit together in a big vessel.

6. In a smaller vessel, combine honey, orange juice, jam, cinnamon, nutmeg, and salt.
7. Mix honey mixture into fruit. Tastes best when given time to marinate in the refrigerator for a few hours.

Exchange List Value:
- Starch 0.5
- Fruit 0.5
- Carbohydrate 0.5

Basic Nutritional Values:
- Calories 95 (Calories from Fat 15)
- Total Fat 2 gm (Saturated Fat 0.3 gm, Trans Fat 0.0 gm, Polyunsaturated Fat 0.3 gm, Monounsaturated Fat 0.7 gm)
- Cholesterol 0 mg
- Sodium 95 mg
- Potassium 125 gm
- Total Carb 21 gm
- Dietary Fiber 2 gm
- Sugars 10 gm
- Protein 2 gm
- Phosphorus 30 gm

Hot Artichoke Dip

Yield: 30 servings, ¼ cup each
Preparation Time: 20 minutes
Chilling Time: 1–4 hours
Ideal slow-cooker size: 4-qt.
Ingredients:

- ¼ cup finely chopped green onions
- 1 cup fat-free mayonnaise
- 1 cup fat-free sour cream
- 1 cup water chestnuts, chopped
- 2 14-oz. jars marinated artichoke hearts, drained
- 2 cups freshly grated Parmesan cheese

Directions:

1. Chop artichoke hearts into small pieces. Put in the mayonnaise, sour cream, water chestnuts, cheese, and green onions. Pour into slow cooker.
2. Cover. Cook on High for about 1–2 hours or on Low for about 3–4 hours.

Serving suggestion:
Serve with crackers or crusty French bread.
Exchange List Value:

- Carbohydrate 0.5
- Fat 0.5

Basic Nutritional Values:

- Calories 57 (Calories from Fat 26)
- Total Fat 3 gm (Saturated Fat 1.2 gm, Polyunsaturated Fat 0.7 gm, Monounsaturated Fat 0.9 gm)
- Cholesterol 6 mg
- Sodium 170 mg
- Total Carb 5 gm
- Dietary Fiber 0 gm
- Sugars 2 gm
- Protein 3 gm

Hot Cheese and Bacon Dip

Yield: 25 servings
Preparation Time: 15 minutes
Chilling Time: 1 hour
Ideal slow-cooker size: 1-qt.
Ingredients:

- ½ tsp. dry mustard
- ½ tsp. salt
- 1 cup fat-free half-and-half
- 1 tsp. dried minced onion
- 2 8-oz. pkgs. fat-free cream cheese, cubed and softened
- 2 tsp. Worcestershire sauce
- 2–3 drops Tabasco sauce
- 8 oz. shredded reduced-fat mild cheddar cheese
- 9 slices bacon, diced

Directions:

1. Brown and drain bacon. Set aside.
2. Combine remaining ingredients in slow cooker.
3. Cover. Cook on Low 1 hour, stirring intermittently until cheese melts.
4. Mix in bacon.

Exchange List Values:

- Lean meat 1.0

Basic Nutritional Values:

- Calories 54 (Calories from Fat 28)
- Total Fat 3 gm (Saturated Fat 1.5 gm, Polyunsaturated Fat 0.2 gm, Monounsaturated Fat 1.1 gm)
- Cholesterol 11 mg
- Sodium 273 mg
- Total Carb 2 gm
- Dietary Fiber 0 gm
- Sugars 1 gm
- Protein 6 gm

Hot Crab Dip

Yield: 20 servings
Preparation Time: 15 minutes
Chilling Time: 3–4 hours
Ideal slow-cooker size: 3- or 4-qt.
Ingredients:

- ⅓ cup salsa
- ½ cup milk
- 1 cup thinly sliced green onions
- 2 8-oz. pkgs. imitation crabmeat, flaked
- 3 8-oz. pkgs. fat-free cream cheese, cubed
- 4-oz. can chopped green chilies
- assorted crackers or bread cubes

Directions:

1. Mix milk and salsa. Move to greased slow cooker.
2. Mix in cream cheese, imitation crabmeat, onions, and chilies.
3. Cover. Cook on Low 3–4 hours, mixing every half an hour.
4. Serve with crackers or bread.

Exchange List Value:

- Carbohydrate 0.5
- Meat, Very Lean 1.0

Basic Nutritional Values:

- Calories 60(Calories from Fat 4)
- Total Fat 0 gm (Saturated Fat 0.1 gm, Polyunsaturated Fat 0.2 gm, Monounsaturated Fat 0.1 gm)
- Cholesterol 9 mg
- Sodium 410 mg
- Total Carb 5 gm
- Dietary Fiber 0 gm
- Sugars 4 gm
- Protein 8 gm

Hot Pizza Dip

Yield: 8 servings
Preparation Time: 20 minutes
Cooking/Baking Time: 5–20 minutes
Ingredients:
- ¼ cup chopped onions, optional
- ¼ cup freshly grated Parmesan cheese, divided
- ¼ tsp. dried basil
- ½ tsp. dried oregano
- ½ tsp. dried parsley
- ½–1 cup pizza sauce
- ¾ cup shredded part-skim mozzarella cheese, divided
- 2 Tbsp. chopped green bell pepper
- 2 Tbsp. sliced black olives, optional
- 8-oz. pkg. fat-free cream cheese, softened

Directions:
1. In a small vessel, mix together cream cheese, oregano, parsley, and basil.
2. Spread mixture on the bottom of greased 9-inch glass pie plate.
3. Drizzle 6 Tbsp. mozzarella and 2 Tbsp. Parmesan cheese on top of cream cheese mixture.
4. Spread the pizza sauce over all.
5. Drizzle with remaining cheese.
6. Sprinkle with green pepper, olives, and onions.
7. Cover and microwave 5 minutes or bake at 350°F for 20 minutes.

Exchange List Value:
- Lean Meat 1.0
- Fat 0.5

Basic Nutritional Values:
- Calories 70 (Calories from Fat 20)

- Total Fat 2.5 gm (Saturated Fat 1.5 gm, Trans Fat 0.0 gm, Polyunsaturated Fat 0.2 gm, Monounsaturated Fat 0.7 gm)
- Cholesterol 15 mg
- Sodium 340 mg
- Potassium 155 gm
- Total Carb 4 gm
- Dietary Fiber 0 gm
- Sugars 2 gm
- Protein 7 gm
- Phosphorus 220 gm

Jalapeño Popper Dip

Yield: 12 servings, approximately ¼ cup per serving
Preparation Time: 15 minutes
Baking Time: 30 minutes
Ingredients:

- ½ cup freshly grated Parmesan cheese
- ½ cup panko bread crumbs
- 1 cup light mayonnaise
- 2 8-oz. pkgs. fat-free cream cheese, softened
- 2-oz. can diced jalapeño peppers, drained
- 4-oz. can chopped green chilies, drained

Directions:

1. Combine cream cheese and mayonnaise in big bowl until smooth. Mix in chilies and peppers.
2. Pour pepper mixture on a greased baking dish.
3. Mix Parmesan and panko. Put on top of pepper mixture.
4. Bake at 350°F for 30 minutes until golden and bubbly.

Serving suggestion:
Serve with veggies, pita chips, or regular corn chips.
Exchange List Values:

- Carbohydrate 0.5
- Lean Meat 1.0
- Fat 0.5

Basic Nutritional Values:

- Calories 105 (Calories from Fat 55)
- Total Fat 6 gm (Saturated Fat 1.2 gm, Trans Fat 0.0 gm, Polyunsaturated Fat 2.7 gm, Monounsaturated Fat 1.6 gm)
- Cholesterol 15 mg
- Sodium 480 mg
- Potassium 130 gm
- Total Carb 6 gm
- Dietary Fiber 0 gm
- Sugars 2 gm

- Protein 6 gm
- Phosphorus 230 gm

Liver Paté

Yield: 12 servings, 2 Tbsp. each
Preparation Time: 20 minutes
Chilling Time: 4–5 hours
Ideal slow-cooker size: 3-qt.
Ingredients:

- ¼ cup light, soft tub margarine
- ¼ tsp. dry mustard
- ¼ tsp. ground ginger
- ½ cup dry wine
- ½ tsp. seasoning salt
- 1 lb. chicken livers
- 1 Tbsp. brandy
- 1 Tbsp. instant minced onion
- 1 Tbsp. light soy sauce
- 1 tsp. instant chicken bouillon
- 1 tsp. minced parsley

Directions:

1. In Crock pot, mix all ingredients except margarine and brandy.
2. Cover. Cook on Low heat for 4–5 hours. Allow to stand in liquid until cool.
3. Drain. Place livers in blender or food grinder. Pour in margarine and brandy. Process until smooth.

Serving suggestion:
Serve with crackers or toast.
Exchange List Value:

- Lean Meat 1.0

Basic Nutritional Values:

- Calories 61 (Calories from Fat 28)
- Total Fat 3 gm (Saturated Fat 0.6 gm, Polyunsaturated Fat 0.6 gm, Monounsaturated Fat 1.2 gm)
- Cholesterol 137 mg

- Sodium 235 mg
- Total Carb 1 gm
- Dietary Fiber 0 gm
- Sugars 0 gm
- Protein 6 gm

Moulded Crab Spread

Yield: 12 servings
Preparation Time: 10 minutes
Chilling Time: 5–7 minutes
Chilling Time: 4 hours
Ingredients:

- 1 cup chopped celery
- 1 cup light mayonnaise
- 10¾-oz. can lower-fat, lower-sodium cream of mushroom soup
- 1-oz. envelope unflavored gelatin
- 2 green onions, chopped
- 3 Tbsp. cold water
- 6-oz. can crab
- 8-oz. fat-free cream cheese, softened

Directions:

1. In a small microwave-safe vessel, drizzle gelatin over cold water. Allow the mixture to stand for about 60 seconds. Microwave uncovered on High heat for about 20 seconds. Mix. Allow it to stand for 1 minute or until gelatin is completely dissolved.
2. In a big saucepan, combine soup, cream cheese, mayonnaise, and gelatin. Cook and stir over medium heat for 5–7 minutes or until smooth.
3. Turn off the heat and add crab, celery, and onions.
4. Move to a 5-cup ring mold, lightly greased. Cover and refrigerate 4 hours or until set.
5. Unmould onto serving platter.

Serving suggestion:
Serve with crackers or bread.
Exchange List Value:

- Carbohydrate 0.5
- Lean Meat 1.0

- Fat 0.5

Basic Nutritional Values:
- Calories 95 (Calories from Fat 45)
- Total Fat 5 gm (Saturated Fat 0.8 gm, Trans Fat 0.0 gm, Polyunsaturated Fat 2.9 gm, Monounsaturated Fat 1.5 gm)
- Cholesterol 20 mg
- Sodium 430 mg
- Potassium 290 gm
- Total Carb 5 gm
- Dietary Fiber 0 gm
- Sugars 2 gm
- Protein 6 gm
- Phosphorus 145 gm

Party Kielbasa

Yield: 48 servings, 1 oz. per serving
Preparation Time: 15 minutes
Cooking/Baking Time: 2–2½ hours
Ingredients:

- ¼ tsp. prepared mustard
- ½ cup brown sugar, packed
- ½ cup chili sauce
- 1 cup ketchup
- 1 Tbsp. lemon juice
- 2 Tbsp. Worcestershire sauce
- 3 lbs. 95%-fat free turkey kielbasa

Directions:

1. Chop the kielbasa or smoked sausage into 6 or 9 big pieces. Lay it in a big pan of water. Simmer for about 20 minutes. Drain. Allow it to Cool slightly. Chop into 1-oz. pieces.
2. Combine all other ingredients in 13x9-inch baking dish. Add kielbasa. Toss to cover with sauce.
3. Bake at 325°F for 1½–2 hours, stirring intermittently.

Exchange List Value:

- Carbohydrate 0.5
- Lean Meat 1.0

Basic Nutritional Values:

- Calories 65 (Calories from Fat 15)
- Total Fat 2 gm (Saturated Fat 0.8 gm, Trans Fat 0.0 gm, Polyunsaturated Fat 0.3 gm, Monounsaturated Fat 0.5 gm)
- Cholesterol 20 mg
- Sodium 380 mg
- Potassium 95 gm
- Total Carb 5 gm
- Dietary Fiber 0 gm
- Sugars 3 gm

- Protein 5 gm
- Phosphorus 55 gm

Party Starter Bean Dip

Yield: 16 servings, ¼ cup per serving
Preparation Time: 20–25 minutes
Baking Time: 20 minutes
Standing Time: 5 minutes
Ingredients:

- 12-oz. jar salsa, divided
- 16-oz. can Old El Paso refried beans or vegetarian refried beans
- 8-oz. pkg. fat-free cream cheese, softened
- nacho tortilla chips

Directions:

1. Spread beans on the bottom of a 9-inch pie pan, spreading up the sides a bit.
2. In a vessel, add cream cheese, then add ⅔ cup salsa and whisk until smooth.
3. Spread cream cheese mixture on beans. Bake for about 20 minutes at 350°F.
4. Spread the residual salsa over dip which has set for 5 minutes.
5. Serve with nacho chips.

Good Side Dishes With This Recipe:
This is nice with a good dish of fruit and assorted snack crackers when eaten as a snack.

Exchange List Value:

- Carbohydrate 0.5

Basic Nutritional Values:

- Calories 40(Calories from Fat 0)
- Total Fat 0 gm(Saturated Fat 0.1 gm, Trans Fat 0.0 gm, Polyunsaturated Fat 0.0 gm, Monounsaturated Fat 0.1 gm)
- Cholesterol 0 mg
- Sodium 345 mg
- Potassium 180 gm

- Total Carb 6 gm
- Dietary Fiber 2 gm
- Sugars 1 gm
- Protein 3 gm
- Phosphorus 105 gm

Pineapple Salsa

Yield: 2½ cups, 10 servings, ¼ cup per serving
Preparation Time: 30 minutes
Ingredients:

- ¼ cup lime juice
- ¼ cup red onion
- ¼ tsp. salt
- 1 cup cucumber
- 1 tsp. garlic
- 1 tsp. grated lime peel
- 1 tsp. sugar
- 1½ cups fresh pineapple
- 2 Tbsp. fresh cilantro
- 2–4 tsp. jalapeño

Directions:

1. Process the ingredients together using a food processor until just chopped.
2. Serve with your favorite tortilla chips.
3. If you don't possess a food processor, you can manually chop the pineapple, cucumber, onion, jalapeño, garlic, and cilantro. Mix with lime juice and peel, sugar, and salt.

Exchange List Value:

- Carbohydrate 0.5

Basic Nutritional Values:

- Calories 20 (Calories from Fat 0)
- Total Fat 0 gm (Saturated Fat 0.0 gm, Trans Fat 0.0 gm, Polyunsaturated Fat 0.0 gm, Monounsaturated Fat 0.0 gm)
- Cholesterol 0 mg
- Sodium 60 mg
- Potassium 55 gm
- Total Carb 5 gm
- Dietary Fiber 1 gm
- Sugars 3 gm

- Protein 0 gm
- Phosphorus 5 gm

Pretty Fruit Kabobs with Dip

Yield: 40 servings, 1 kabob and 2 Tbsp. dip per serving
Preparation Time: 30 minutes
Ingredients:
- ¼ cup fat-free milk
- 1 honeydew, cut in 80 pieces
- 1 lb. green grapes
- 1 lb. red grapes
- 1 pineapple, cut in 80 pieces
- 1 tsp. vanilla extract
- 2 lbs. strawberries, cut in 40 pieces
- 40 8-inch skewers
- 6 oz. marshmallow cream
- 8-oz. Neufchâtel (⅓-less-fat) cream cheese, softened
- 9-oz. fat-free frozen whipped topping, thawed

Directions:
1. Stir cream cheese until fluffy.
2. Fold in whipped topping and marshmallow cream. Pour in vanilla and milk.
3. Refrigerate until time to serve.
4. To make the kabobs, thread green grape, pineapple, red grape, honeydew, strawberry, honeydew, red grape, pineapple, green grape on skewers. Serve.

Notes:
A bright, and yummy combo! Fresh fruit is always a big winner, especially if there are guests with diet restraints.

Exchange List Value:
- Fruit 0.5
- Carbohydrate 0.5

Basic Nutritional Values:
- Calories 80 (Calories from Fat 15)
- Total Fat 2 gm (Saturated Fat 0.8 gm, Trans Fat 0.0 gm, Polyunsaturated Fat 0.1 gm, Monounsaturated Fat 0.3 gm)

- Cholesterol 5 mg
- Sodium 40 mg
- Potassium 175 gm
- Total Carb 16 gm
- Dietary Fiber 1 gm
- Sugars 12 gm
- Protein 1 gm
- Phosphorus 30 gm

Quick and Easy Nacho Dip

Yield: 20 servings
Preparation Time: 15 minutes
Chilling Time: 2 hours
Ideal slow-cooker size: 3-qt.
Ingredients:

- ½ lb. 85%-lean ground beef
- 1½ cups fat-free sour cream
- 1½ cups shredded reduced-fat sharp cheddar cheese, divided
- 15-oz. can fat-free refried beans
- 2 16-oz. jars salsa (as hot or mild as you like)
- 2 cloves garlic, minced, optional
- onion powder, optional
- pepper, optional
- tortilla chips

Directions:

1. Brown the ground beef. Drain. Put in pepper, onion powder, and minced garlic, if you want.
2. Mix beef, salsa, beans, sour cream, and 1 cup cheese in Crock pot.
3. Cover. Heat on Low 2 hours. Just before serving, drizzle with ½ cup cheese.
4. Serve with tortilla chips.

Exchange List Value:

- Carbohydrate 0.5
- Lean Meat 1.0

Basic Nutritional Values:

- Calories 80 (Calories from Fat 27)
- Total Fat 3 gm (Saturated Fat 1.5 gm, Polyunsaturated Fat 0.2 gm, Monounsaturated Fat 1.0 gm)
- Cholesterol 14 mg
- Sodium 298 mg

- Total Carb 8 gm
- Dietary Fiber 2 gm
- Sugars 3 gm
- Protein 6 gm

Reuben Appetizer Squares

Yield: 24 servings, 2-inch square per serving
Preparation Time: 20 minutes
Baking Time: 12–15 minutes
Ingredients:

- ½ cup fat-free milk
- ⅔ cup light mayonnaise
- 1 cup sauerkraut, well drained
- 1 Tbsp. ketchup
- 1 Tbsp. pickle relish
- 1½ cups reduced-fat shredded Swiss cheese (approximately 6 oz.)
- 2 cups baking mix
- 2 Tbsp. vegetable oil
- 2½-oz. pkg. thinly sliced smoked corned beef, coarsely chopped

Directions:

1. Combine baking mix, milk, and oil until soft dough forms. Press into ungreased 9x13-inch baking pan.
2. Sprinkle the sauerkraut and corned beef on top.
3. Combine mayonnaise, relish, and ketchup; spread over corned beef. Drizzle with cheese.
4. Bake at 450°F until cheese is bubbly and crust is golden brown, 12–15 minutes.
5. Slice into 2-inch squares.

Exchange List Value:

- Starch 0.5
- Fat 1.0

Basic Nutritional Values:

- Calories 90 (Calories from Fat 45)
- Total Fat 5 gm (Saturated Fat 1.1 gm, Trans Fat 0.0 gm, Polyunsaturated Fat 1.4 gm, Monounsaturated Fat 1.9 gm)
- Cholesterol 5 mg

- Sodium 250 mg
- Potassium 45 gm
- Total Carb 8 gm
- Dietary Fiber 1 gm
- Sugars 2 gm
- Protein 4 gm
- Phosphorus 110 gm

Reuben Spread

Yield: 52 servings
Preparation Time: 15 minutes
Chilling Time: 1–2 hours
Ideal slow-cooker size: 3-qt.
Ingredients:
- ½ lb. corned beef, shredded or chopped, all visible fat removed
- 1 cup mayonnaise
- 1 cup shredded cheddar cheese
- 1 cup shredded Swiss cheese
- 16-oz. can sauerkraut, well drained
- bread slices
- Thousand Island dressing, optional

Directions:
1. Mix all ingredients except bread and Thousand Island dressing in Crock pot. Combine thoroughly.
2. Cover. Cook on High heat 1–2 hours until heated through, stirring intermittently.
3. Reduce heat to Low and keep warm in cooker while serving. Apply the spread to bread slices. Top individual servings with Thousand Island dressing, if you want.

Notes:
Low-fat cheese and mayonnaise are not recommended for this spread.

Variation:
Use dried beef instead of corned beef.

Exchange List Value:
- Fat 1.0

Basic Nutritional Values:
- Calories 58 (Calories from Fat 49)
- Total Fat 5 gm (Saturated Fat 1.5 gm, Polyunsaturated Fat 1.9 gm, Monounsaturated Fat 1.6 gm)

- Cholesterol 10 mg
- Sodium 113 mg
- Total Carb 1 gm
- Dietary Fiber 0 gm
- Sugars 0 gm
- Protein 2 gm

Roasted Pepper and Artichoke Spread

Yield: 24 servings
Preparation Time: 20 minutes
Chilling Time: 1 hour
Ideal slow-cooker size: 1-qt.
Ingredients:

- ⅓ cup finely chopped roasted red bell pepper
- ½ cup reduced-fat mayonnaise
- 1 clove garlic, minced
- 1 cup grated Parmesan cheese
- 14-oz. can artichoke hearts, drained and chopped finely
- 8-oz. pkg. fat-free cream cheese, softened
- crackers, cut-up fresh vegetables, or snack-bread slices

Directions:

1. Mix Parmesan cheese, mayonnaise, cream cheese, and garlic in food processor. Process until smooth. Place mixture in Crock pot.
2. Add artichoke hearts and red bell pepper. Mix well.
3. Cover. Cook on Low 1 hour. Mix again.
4. Use as spread for crackers, chop-up fresh vegetables, or snack-bread slices.

Exchange List Value:

- Fat 1.0

Basic Nutritional Values:

- Calories 49 (Calories from Fat 29)
- Total Fat 3 gm (Saturated Fat 1.3 gm, Polyunsaturated Fat 0.7 gm, Monounsaturated Fat 0.9 gm)
- Cholesterol 8 mg
- Sodium 209 mg
- Total Carb 2 gm
- Dietary Fiber 0 gm
- Sugars 1 gm
- Protein 4 gm

Sesame Chicken Wings

Yield: 16 appetizer servings
Preparation Time: 40 minutes
Chilling Time: 2½–5 hours
Ideal slow-cooker size: 4-qt.
Ingredients:

- ½ cup no-salt-added ketchup
- ¾ cup light soy sauce
- 1 cup honey
- 2 cloves garlic, minced
- 2 Tbsp. canola oil
- 2 Tbsp. sesame oil
- 3 lbs. chicken wings
- pepper, to taste
- salt, to taste
- sugar substitute to equal 6 Tbsp. sugar
- toasted sesame seeds

Directions:

1. Wash the wings. Chop at joint. Drizzle with salt and pepper. Lay on broiler pan.
2. Broil 5 inches from top, 10 minutes on both sides each. Place chicken in Crock pot.
3. Mix remaining ingredients except sesame seeds. Pour on chicken.
4. Cover. Cook on Low heat for about 5 hours or High 2½ hours.
5. Drizzle sesame seeds over top immediately before serving.

Exchange List Value:

- Carbohydrate 1.5
- Meat, High Fat 1.0

Basic Nutritional Values:

- Calories 192 (Calories from Fat 77)

- Total Fat 9 gm (Saturated Fat 1.8 gm, Polyunsaturated Fat 2.3 gm, Monounsaturated Fat 3.7 gm)
- Cholesterol 22 mg
- Sodium 453 mg
- Total Carb 21 gm
- Dietary Fiber 0 gm
- Sugars 21 gm
- Protein 9 gm

Shrimp Dip

Yield: 1½ cups, 9 servings, 2 Tbsp. per serving
Preparation Time: 15 minutes
Chilling Time: 1 hour
Ingredients:
- ½ cup cooked shrimp, finely chopped
- 1 cup fat-free sour cream
- 1-oz. pkg. Italian salad dressing mix
- 2 Tbsp. green pepper, finely chopped
- 2 tsp. lemon juice
- 3-oz. pkg. Neufchâtel (⅓-less-fat) cream cheese, softened

Directions:
1. Mix all ingredients together.
2. Chill for at least 60 minutes.
3. Serve with chips or crackers.

Exchange List Value:
- Carbohydrate 0.5
- Fat 0.5

Basic Nutritional Values:
- Calories 65 (Calories from Fat 20)
- Total Fat 2.5 gm (Saturated Fat 1.4 gm, Trans Fat 0.0 gm, Polyunsaturated Fat 0.1 gm, Monounsaturated Fat 0.6 gm)
- Cholesterol 25 mg
- Sodium 385 mg
- Potassium 70 gm
- Total Carb 7 gm
- Dietary Fiber 0 gm
- Sugars 3 gm
- Protein 4 gm
- Phosphorus 65 gm

Slow-Cooked Salsa

Yield: 34 servings, ¼ cup each
Preparation Time: 15–20 minutes
Chilling Time: 3 hours
Ideal slow-cooker size: 3-qt.
Ingredients:

- ¼ cup cilantro leaves
- ½ tsp. salt
- 1 onion, chopped
- 10 fresh Roma, or plum, tomatoes, chopped coarsely
- 2 cloves garlic, minced
- 2 jalapeño peppers

Directions:

1. Put the tomatoes, garlic, and onion in slow cooker.
2. Eliminate stems from jalapeños. Eliminate the seeds, too, if you prefer a milder flavor. Slice the jalapeños. Mix into slow cooker.
3. Cover. Cook on High heat for 150-180 minutes, or until vegetables are softened.
4. Let it cool.
5. When cooled, mix cooked mixture with cilantro and salt in a blender or food processor. Blend or process to the consistency that you prefer.

Exchange List Value:

• Free Food

Basic Nutritional Values:

- Calories 10 (Calories from Fat 0)
- Total Fat 0 gm (Saturated Fat 0 gm, Polyunsaturated Fat 0 gm Monounsaturated Fat 0 gm Cholesterol 0 mg),
- Sodium 35 mg
- Total Carb 2 gm
- Dietary Fiber 0 gm
- Sugars 1 gm

- Protein 0 gm

Smoky Barbecue Meatballs
Yield: 10 servings, 1 meatball per serving
Preparation Time: 30 minutes
Baking Time: 50–60 minutes
Ingredients:
- ¼ cup egg substitute
- ¼ tsp. chili powder
- ¼ tsp. garlic powder
- ¼ tsp. pepper
- ¼–½ cup finely chopped onion, optional
- ½ cup fat-free evaporated milk or milk
- ½ cup quick oats
- 1 tsp. salt
- 1½ lbs. 90%-lean ground beef

Directions:
1. Bring the sauce to a boil and boil for approximately 2 minutes.
2. Save a little before pouring over the meatballs. Then, at the end of baking and just before serving, brush on the saved sauce.

Making the Sauce:
Ingredients:
- ¼ cup chopped onion
- ¼ tsp. liquid smoke
- 1 cup ketchup
- 6 Tbsp. Splenda Brown Sugar Blend

Directions:
1. Combine beef, oats, milk, egg substitute, onion, garlic powder, pepper, chili powder, and salt together. Form 10 balls, each weighing approximately 2 oz. Place in 9x13-oz baking dish.
2. Bake at 350°F for 40 minutes. Combine the sauce ingredients while the meatballs bake. Set aside.

3. Eliminate any grease from the meatballs after they have baked for approximately 40 minutes. Pour sauce over meatballs.
4. Bake meatballs and sauce another 10–20 minutes, until bubbling and heated completely.

Exchange List Value:
- Carbohydrate 1.0
- Lean Meat 2.0
- Fat 0.5

Basic Nutritional Values:
- Calories 190 (Calories from Fat 55)
- Total Fat 6 gm (Saturated Fat 2.3 gm, Trans Fat 0.3 gm, Polyunsaturated Fat 0.3 gm, Monounsaturated Fat 2.4 gm)
- Cholesterol 40 mg
- Sodium 450 mg
- Potassium 375 gm
- Total Carb 18 gm
- Dietary Fiber 1 gm
- Sugars 11 gm
- Protein 16 gm
- Phosphorus 170 gm

Spinach Roll-Ups

Yield: 23 servings, 3 roll-ups per serving
Preparation Time: 30 minutes
Chilling Time: 12 hours
Ingredients:

- ¼ cup water chestnuts, chopped
- 1 cup fat-free sour cream
- 1 cup light mayonnaise
- 1 pkg. ranch dressing mix
- 2 10-oz. boxes frozen spinach, thawed and drained
- 2 oz. bacon bits (half of a small jar)
- 6 green onions, chopped
- 7 10-inch tortillas

Directions:

1. Combine together ingredients except tortillas.
2. Coat the top of the tortillas with the mixture. Roll up and lock with toothpicks.
3. Refrigerate overnight. Cut into 1-inch pieces to serve.

Exchange List Value:

- Starch 1.0
- Fat 1.0

Basic Nutritional Values:

- Calories 120 (Calories from Fat 45)
- Total Fat 5 gm (Saturated Fat 1.2 gm, Trans Fat 0.0 gm, Polyunsaturated Fat 1.8 gm, Monounsaturated Fat 1.7 gm)
- Cholesterol 5 mg
- Sodium 440 mg
- Potassium 160 gm
- Total Carb 15 gm
- Dietary Fiber 2 gm
- Sugars 1 gm
- Protein 4 gm
- Phosphorus 50 gm

Strawberry Yogurt Dip

Yield: 5½ cups, 22 servings, ¼ cup per serving
Preparation Time: 20 minutes
Ingredients:
- 1–1½ cups mashed strawberries, fresh or thawed frozen
- 2 6-oz. cartons light strawberry yogurt
- 8-oz. frozen light whipped topping, thawed
- sliced fruit

Directions:
1. Mix whipped topping, yogurt, and mashed berries.
2. Serve with an assortment of sliced fresh fruit.

Exchange List Value:
- Carbohydrate 0.5

Basic Nutritional Values:
- Calories 35 (Calories from Fat 15)
- Total Fat 2 gm (Saturated Fat 1.2 gm, Trans Fat 0.0 gm, Polyunsaturated Fat 0.0 gm, Monounsaturated Fat 0.1 gm)
- Cholesterol 0 mg
- Sodium 15 mg
- Potassium 45 gm
- Total Carb 6 gm
- Dietary Fiber 0 gm
- Sugars 5 gm
- Protein 1 gm
- Phosphorus 25 gm

Stuffed Mushrooms

Yield: 10 servings, 2 mushroom caps per serving
Preparation Time: 25 minutes
Baking Time: 20–30 minutes
Ingredients:

- ¼ cup freshly grated Parmesan cheese
- ¼ cup trans-fat-free tub margarine
- ½ cup Italian seasoned bread crumbs
- 2 Tbsp. finely chopped onion
- 2 Tbsp. oil
- 20 fresh mushrooms, approximately 1 lb.

Directions:

1. Clean the mushrooms; remove stems but save them for later. Put the mushrooms in greased baking pan, stem-side up.
2. Thinly slice 2 tablespoons of the mushroom stems. Eliminate the rest. Sauté onion and chopped mushroom stems in margarine. Remove from heat heat and mix in the crumbs.
3. Fill each mushroom cap with the mixture. Drizzle Parmesan cheese over all. Drizzle with oil.
4. Bake at 350°F for 20–30 minutes.

Exchange List Value:

- Carbohydrate 0.5
- Fat 1.5

Basic Nutritional Values:

- Calories 90 (Calories from Fat 65)
- Total Fat 7 gm (Saturated Fat 1.5 gm, Trans Fat 0.0 gm, Polyunsaturated Fat 1.8 gm, Monounsaturated Fat 3.3 gm)
- Cholesterol 0 mg
- Sodium 150 mg
- Potassium 145 gm
- Total Carb 6 gm

- Dietary Fiber 1 gm
- Sugars 1 gm
- Protein 3 gm
- Phosphorus 55 gm

Sweet Cheese Ball

Yield: 35 servings, 2 Tbsp. per serving
Preparation Time: 10 minutes
Chilling Time: 4 hours
Ingredients:
- 1 cup sliced almonds
- 15-oz. can fruit cocktail, well drained
- 2 8-oz. pkgs. fat-free cream cheese, softened
- 3.4-oz. pkg. French vanilla instant pudding mix
- 4 Tbsp. orange juice

Directions:
1. Combine cream cheese, pudding, fruit, and juice.
2. Refrigerate to set up, about 4 hours.
3. Mould into a ball and roll in almonds.
4. Place in refrigerator until ready to serve.

Serving suggestion:
Serve with buttery crackers such as Town House, graham crackers, or apple slices.

Exchange List Value:
- Carbohydrate 0.5

Basic Nutritional Values:
- Calories 40 (Calories from Fat 15)
- Total Fat 2 gm (Saturated Fat 0.1 gm, Trans Fat 0.0 gm, Polyunsaturated Fat 0.3 gm, Monounsaturated Fat 0.8 gm)
- Cholesterol 0 mg
- Sodium 120 mg
- Potassium 65 gm
- Total Carb 5 gm
- Dietary Fiber 0 gm
- Sugars 3 gm
- Protein 2 gm
- Phosphorus 100 gm

Taco Appetizer Platter

Yield: 15 servings, approximately 1½ oz. per serving
Preparation Time: 20 minutes
Chilling Time: 10 minutes
Ingredients:

- ¼ cup fat-free milk
- ½ cup honey barbecue sauce
- ½ cup water
- 1 cup chopped green onions
- 1 cup shredded 75%-less-fat cheddar cheese
- 1 lb. 90%-lean ground beef
- 2 8-oz. pkgs. cream cheese, softened
- 2 medium tomatoes, seeded and chopped
- 4-oz. can chopped green chilies, drained
- 7 tsp. salt-free taco seasoning
- corn chips
- lettuce, optional

Directions:

1. Using a skillet, cook beef over moderate heat until no longer pink. Drain. Pour in water and add the taco seasoning; simmer for 5 minutes.
2. In a vessel, mix the cream cheese and milk; spread on 14-inch serving platter or pizza pan. Add a layer of meat mixture on top. Drizzle with chilies, tomatoes, and onions. Put in the lettuce, if you want.
3. Sprinkle with barbecue sauce. Drizzle with cheddar cheese. Serve with corn chips.

Exchange List Value:

- Carbohydrate 0.5
- Lean Meat 2.0

Basic Nutritional Values:

- Calories 115 (Calories from Fat 30)

- Total Fat 4 gm (Saturated Fat 1.4 gm, Trans Fat 0.2 gm, Polyunsaturated Fat 0.2 gm, Monounsaturated Fat 1.2 gm)
- Cholesterol 25 mg
- Sodium 350 mg
- Potassium 285 gm
- Total Carb 7 gm
- Dietary Fiber 1 gm
- Sugars 5 gm
- Protein 12 gm
- Phosphorus 260 gm

Texas Caviar

Yield: 7½ cups, 30 servings, ¼ cup per serving
Preparation Time: 15 minutes
Chilling Time: 10 minutes
Chilling Time: 12–24 hours
Ingredients:

- ¼ cup oil
- ½ cup sugar
- ¾ cup apple cider vinegar
- 1 Tbsp. water
- 15½-oz. can black beans, rinsed
- 15½-oz. can black-eyed peas, rinsed
- 2 11-oz. cans white shoepeg corn
- 8-oz. jar chopped pimento
- salt and pepper, to taste
- small green bell pepper, finely diced
- small red onion, chopped

Directions:

1. In saucepan, mix sugar, oil, salt, pepper, vinegar, and water. Heat until boiling, then allow to cool.
2. Combine together peas, corn, beans, pimento, green pepper, and onion. Put the cooked sauce over mixture. Mix. Serve cold.
3. Preferably, refrigerate 24 hours before serving.
4. Serve with scoop Fritos or corn chips.

Exchange List Value:

- Starch 0.5
- Fat 0.5

Basic Nutritional Values:

- Calories 70 (Calories from Fat 20)
- Total Fat 2 gm (Saturated Fat 0.2 gm, Trans Fat 0.0 gm, Polyunsaturated Fat 0.6 gm, Monounsaturated Fat 1.2 gm)
- Cholesterol 0 mg

- Sodium 85 mg
- Potassium 125 gm
- Total Carb 11 gm
- Dietary Fiber 2 gm
- Sugars 4 gm
- Protein 2 gm
- Phosphorus 40 gm

Tex-Mex Eggs

Ingredients:

- ¼ cup fat-free plain yogurt or light mayonnaise
- ¼ tsp. salt
- 1 Tbsp. finely diced onion
- 1 tsp. lemon juice
- 1 tsp. prepared mustard
- 1 tsp. taco seasoning
- 6 big eggs, hard-boiled and peeled

Directions:

To hard-boil eggs:

1. Put eggs in a single layer in a lidded pan.
2. Pour cold water into the pan until the eggs are covered completely.
3. Cover the pan and bring to a full broil.
4. Just as the water begins the full boil, instantly turn the heat down to low for a simmer. Let it barely simmer for exactly 18 minutes.
5. Turn off the heat, eliminate the hot water, and pour in cold water to cool the eggs.

To make deviled eggs:

1. Slice the eggs in half lengthwise. Carefully take out the yolk sections into a vessel.
2. Eliminate two yolks if using a recipe for 6; Eliminate 4 yolks if using a recipe for 12. Mash the rest of the yolk sections together using a fork. Mix in the rest of the ingredients with yolk mixture until smooth.
3. Fill the vacant egg whites. The filling will look like a little mound in the egg white. Garnish, if you wish.
4. Refrigerate.

Exchange List Value:

• Med-Fat Meat 1.0

Basic Nutritional Values:

- Calories 60 (Calories from Fat 30)
- Total Fat 4 gm (Saturated Fat 1.1 gm, Trans Fat 0.0 gm, Polyunsaturated Fat 0.7 gm, Monounsaturated Fat 1.2 gm)
- Cholesterol 125 mg
- Sodium 215 mg
- Potassium 95 gm
- Total Carb 2 gm
- Dietary Fiber 0 gm
- Sugars 1 gm
- Protein 6 gm
- Phosphorus 90 gm

Veggie Pizza

Yield: 18 servings, 2x3-inch rectangle per serving
Preparation Time: 20–30 minutes
Chilling Time: 9–12 minutes
Chilling Time: 30 minutes
Ingredients:

- ½ cup fat-free mayonnaise
- ½ cup finely chopped sweet onion or red onion
- ½ cup sliced ripe olives
- ½ tsp. onion salt
- ¾ cup cheddar cheese, shredded fine, optional
- ¾–1 cup broccoli florets
- ¾–1 cup finely chopped green pepper or mushrooms
- ¾–1 cup finely chopped tomato, membranes and seeds removed
- 1 tsp. dill weed
- 2 8-oz. pkgs. refrigerated crescent rolls
- 8-oz. pkg. fat-free cream cheese, softened

Directions:

1. Divide the dough into 4 rectangles.
2. Press onto bottom and up sides of 10x13-inch jelly roll baking pan to make the crust.
3. Bake for 9–12 minutes at 350°F or until golden brown. Allow it to cool.
4. Combine cream cheese, mayonnaise, dill, and onion salt until thoroughly mixed.
5. Spread over cooled crust, but keep the thickness to medium-low.
6. Top with cut vegetables and optional cheese.
7. Press down gently into cream cheese mixture.
8. Place in the refrigerator. Chop into squares to serve.

Exchange List Value:

- Starch 1.0

- Fat 1.0

Basic Nutritional Values:

- Calories 130 (Calories from Fat 65)
- Total Fat 7 gm (Saturated Fat 1.5 gm, Trans Fat 0.0 gm, Polyunsaturated Fat 0.8 gm, Monounsaturated Fat 4.1 gm)
- Cholesterol 0 mg
- Sodium 400 mg
- Potassium 110 gm
- Total Carb 12 gm
- Dietary Fiber 1 gm
- Sugars 3 gm
- Protein 3 gm
- Phosphorus 150 gm

Yummy Barbecue Wings

Yield: 8–10 servings
Preparation Time: 30 minutes
Broiling Time: 16 minutes
Chilling Time: 4–6 hours
Ideal slow-cooker size: 3-qt.
Ingredients:

- ½ cup barbecue sauce
- 12-oz. jar no sugar added or sugar-free grape jelly
- 2 Tbsp. Dijon mustard
- 4 lbs. chicken wings, cut at the joint, tips removed and discarded
- pepper, to taste
- salt, to taste

Directions:

1. Preheat your oven to a low broil.
2. Place your wing pieces on a baking sheet and drizzle both sides with salt and pepper. Place them under the broiler for approximately 8 minutes on each side.
3. As the wings broil, combine together the remaining ingredients.
4. When your wings are done under the broiler, Put them into a greased slow cooker.
5. Pour the sauce you just mixed over the top, and toss the wings around using tongs to make sure they are completely coated with sauce.
6. Cook on Low for approximately 4–6 hours.

Exchange List Value:

- Fruit 1.0
- Med-Fat Meat 4.0
- Fat 0

Basic Nutritional Values:

- Calories 369 (Calories from Fat 167)

- Total Fat 18.6 gm (Saturated Fat 9 gm, Trans Fat 0.2 gm, Polyunsaturated Fat 3.6 gm, Monounsaturated Fat 8.5 gm)
- Cholesterol 138 mg
- Sodium 544 mg
- Potassium 428 gm
- Total Carb 4.7 gm
- Dietary Fiber 0.4 gm
- Sugars 18.6gm
- Protein 30.9 gm
- Phosphorus 227 gm

Endnote

Thank you for reading my book and getting this far. Sadly, this is all that there is to this book. However, there are many more books in the "Diabetic's Delight" series. If you liked this book, you'll love them. Just do a search on amazon and you'll find them. Also, your feedback is greatly valued. Please leave a review for this book on amazon so I can improve this book, and other books in the series.

Goodbyes are hard, but nothing lasts forever. So, good luck, and have fun!

Made in the USA
San Bernardino, CA
13 December 2019